Bicentennial

Plays and Programs

A collection of royalty-free plays, playlets,
choral readings & poems for young people

By
AILEEN FISHER

Publishers   **PLAYS, INC.**   *Boston*

11,710

Library of Congress Cataloging in Publication Data

Main entry under title.

Bicentennial plays and programs.

SUMMARY: Includes one-act plays, poems, choral readings, and other material on bicentennial themes for presentation by school and amateur groups.
1. Amateur theatricals. 2. United States--History--Drama. (1. Amateur theatricals.
2. United States--History--Drama) I. Fisher, Aileen Lucia, 1906 -
PN6120.H5B5   812'.008'031   75-9744
ISBN 0-8238-0185-3

CONTENTS

Preface

Two hundred years is not a long time in the history of civilization. But it is a crowded and exciting span of years in the history of the United States of America.

Had it not been for a determined taxation policy on the part of England, and for an exceptional array of patriotic talent in colonial America after the end of the French and Indian War in 1763, our nation might never have been born. It might have remained a part of the British empire. As it was, the indignation of the colonists against the British tax policy led to the adoption of the rallying cry, "No taxation without representation." Town meetings were held; Sons of Liberty were organized in protest.

Colonial opposition came to a head in December, 1773, when patriots disguised as Indians dumped tea from three British vessels into Boston harbor. The storm broke. England closed Boston harbor to shipping and quartered troops in the city. Patriots got out their muskets. George Washington proposed raising an army of a thousand men at his own expense and marching to the relief of Boston.

Officially the American Revolution began on April 19, 1775, when the first shots were fired at Lexington and Concord. The next year we declared our independence, not as thirteen loosely organized colonies, but as a newly born nation of thirteen states, the United States of America.

We declared our independence... yet for seven grueling

years we had to fight to make it a reality. At the time of the signing of the Declaration, John Adams said: "I am well aware of the Toil and Blood and Treasure that it will cost to maintain this Declaration and support and defend these States." How right he was!

In two hundred years the appearance of our country and our way of life have changed a great deal. But our ideal of life, liberty, and the pursuit of happiness has not changed. No political philosophy has ever worked so well in the history of mankind as our philosophy of government "of the people, by the people, and for the people." We can look back with boundless gratitude at the foresight and genius of the Founding Fathers and all the nameless ragged Continentals who fought to make freedom more than just a dream.

Here in the pages that follow is a sort of panorama of events that attended the birth of our nation, and a compendium of ideals that the colonists fought and died for. Here is a look at a young country whose ideals of freedom are still flourishing, giving hope to people everywhere that some day liberty and justice will prevail throughout a unified world.

April, 1975   —A.F.

Our Great Declaration

(*A play in radio style*)

Characters

NARRATOR

JEFFERSON

BOY

GIRL

CHORUS

WASHINGTON

FRANKLIN

PRIME MINISTER

AGENTS

MEN

WOMEN

PATRICK HENRY

WILLIAM PITT

TOWN CRIER

JOHN ADAMS

READER

JOHN DICKINSON

JOHN DUNLAP

HELPER

ABIGAIL ADAMS

JOHN QUINCY ADAMS,
   age nine

SONS OF LIBERTY

MRS. JACKSON

HUGH JACKSON

ANDREW JACKSON, *age nine*

LINCOLN

NARRATOR: This is the story of the noblest document in the history of our country—the Declaration of Independence. It is not a long document. You can read it aloud in fifteen minutes, including the names of the fifty-six signers. Leaving out the recital of grievances, you can read it in less than five minutes . . . words that are as stirring and full of meaning now as when

7

they were first penned in that hot Philadelphia summer of 1776! Think of Thomas Jefferson, a young lawyer of thirty-three, sitting in a stuffy lodging-house room, trying to figure out those words.

JEFFERSON: How can I write this down so it will carry conviction? What I want to say is that governments are established to secure the liberty and happiness of the people, all people—not just a favored few. When a government shows a determination to rob the people of their rights, it is their duty to overthrow that government and establish another that assures them liberty and safety. "When in the course of human events . . ."

NARRATOR: Jefferson finished the first draft in two days. Only two days to compose a document that stands as one of the greatest in the history of the English-speaking world! The parchment, once so fresh and bright with new ink upon it, is faded now. But the ringing challenge is still there . . . even as the message of liberty still speaks from the long-silent Liberty Bell that pealed out during the celebration of the adoption of the Declaration. (*Sound of bell*)

LOUDSPEAKER: "Proclaim liberty throughout all the land and unto all the inhabitants thereof." (*Sound of bell*)

NARRATOR: Liberty! The keyword of the great Declaration.

JEFFERSON: "We hold these truths to be self-evident, that all men are created equal, that they are endowed by their Creator with certain unalienable Rights, that among these are Life, Liberty, and the pursuit of Happiness."

NARRATOR: Twice the Declaration was whisked out of harm's way during the Revolutionary War. Twice it was almost burned. It was almost captured by the British in the War of 1812. But now the historic document is safe. Any time you go to Washington, D.C., you can see it in its shrine in the National Archives Building sealed in a bronze and glass case and ready to be lowered at a moment's notice into one of the strongest safes in the world.

BOY (*Eagerly*): There it is standing up in the case! "The Unanimous Declaration of the thirteen United States of America." It's funny handwriting, isn't it? Not the kind we learn in school.

GIRL: I think it's beautiful writing.

BOY: But hard to read. Some of the words are so dim I can scarcely make them out. And look at those signatures.

GIRL: They're blurred because that's where the parchment was rolled and unrolled so often.

BOY: Say, look at that first *s* in *necessary*. Just like an *f*. "When in the course of human events it becomes nec-ef-sary . . ." If I didn't know the words, I'd have a hard time making them out.

GIRL: Look at John Hancock's signature. Big as life right in the middle, at the top. Nobody could miss it.

BOY: He wrote it big on purpose . . . so King George could read it without spectacles and know that the richest man in the colonies was for independence!

GIRL (*Thoughtfully*): I wonder what it was like then, way back when there were thirteen colonies standing together for independence.

NARRATOR: You wonder what it was like then? Well, you have to go back a long way in time—back to the days when we weren't singing "My Country 'Tis of Thee," but "God Save the King"—King George, the Third.

CHORUS:

> "God save our gracious King,
> Long live our noble King,
> God save the King!
> Send him victorious,
> Happy and glorious,
> Long to reign over us,
> God save the King!"

NARRATOR: Long to reign over us! We can't imagine, of course, how it felt to have a king reign over us. But in the middle of the eighteenth century the King meant a great deal to the colonists. All through the troubles that led to the war with England, the colonists kept hoping that Parliament would give in and remedy their grievances. Even as late as 1774 George Washington said . . .

WASHINGTON: I am well satisfied that no such thing as independence is desired by any thinking man in all North America. I abhor the idea of separation.

NARRATOR: And about the same time Benjamin Franklin said . . .

FRANKLIN: Whatever else the Americans might desire, they do not want independence.

NARRATOR: Before the Revolution, most of the colonists had a feeling of pride in being part of the great British empire. They did not want the tie broken. They merely wanted to have their rights as Englishmen respected. If this had been done, who knows, we might still be singing "God Save the King" instead of "America." (CHORUS *sings first stanza of "America."*)

CHORUS:

> "My country 'tis of thee, (*Etc.*)

NARRATOR: Trouble started brewing after the end of the

French and Indian War in 1763. Up to that time the colonists had been fairly well satisfied with English rule. True, Parliament had tried to control colonial trade by levying taxes on imports. But England was too busy fighting long wars to enforce the tax laws. It was only after England emerged victorious, that she could turn her full attention to the colonies. In the winter of 1763-4, the Prime Minister of England called together the agents of the colonies:

PRIME MINISTER: Gentlemen, the time has come when we should be getting substantial revenue from America. Our long-drawn-out wars with the French and Indians have been costly. I propose that a specific sum be levied on the colonies, to be paid yearly.

AGENT: May I interrupt, Mr. Prime Minister. I am certain that levying a specific demand on the colonies for revenue will lead to the direst consequences. The Americans will not stand for it, sir.

OTHER AGENTS: Aye. Aye.

PRIME MINISTER: Perhaps a stamp tax, then. We must have revenue, gentlemen. I shall propose at the coming session of Parliament that a stamp duty be levied on the colonies. Or if not a stamp tax at first, then some other tax, on imports, say.

NARRATOR: In 1764 Parliament passed the Sugar Act, levying a tax on certain colonial imports including sugar. Up and down the Atlantic seaboard outraged colonists objected and petitioned for repeal. But Parliament stood firm. Early the next year it passed the Stamp Act. In all, fifty-five articles were taxed. Opposition raged like a prairie fire throughout the colonies.

1ST MAN: Dig down in our pockets and pay for stamps to be pasted on legal papers and the like! Not on your life.

NARRATOR: A tax on tea—the drink loved by all colonists of English ancestry! Indignation against the tax led to the Boston Tea Party in December, 1773, when citizens of Boston, disguised as Indians, dumped chests of tea from three British vessels into the harbor. Parliament retaliated immediately.

TOWN CRIER: Hear ye, hear ye, hear ye—as a result of the Boston Tea Party, Parliament has enacted new laws to punish the colonists. The port of Boston is closed to all trade by sea! Town meetings are subject to the control of the English governor! British troops are to be quartered in Massachusetts towns! Hear ye, hear ye, hear ye!

NARRATOR: Indignation at the treatment of Boston swept from one end of the colonies to the other. Paul Revere rode the three hundred and fifty miles to Philadelphia on horseback to spread the news. Soon help began coming in from all quarters—rice from South Carolina, money and flour from Virginia, flocks of sheep from Connecticut. In the Virginia Convention of July, 1774, George Washington stood up and made a startling proposal . . .

WASHINGTON: I will raise one thousand men, subsist them at my own expense, and march myself at their head for the relief of Boston.

NARRATOR: A few rash patriots even began to talk of independence, of separation from England.

1ST MAN: Instead of fighting for the restoration of our privileges, let us fight for freedom and independence.

2ND MAN: Independence? Who wants independence? All we want is justice and an end to tyranny.

NARRATOR: Colonists were eager to show their sympathy with Boston, so they were glad when Virginia called for a Congress of all the colonies. The first Continental

Congress met at Philadelphia. It drew up a Declaration of Rights and Grievances, and to put teeth into it, declared a boycott on British goods. John Adams, a delegate to the Congress from Massachusetts, wrote to his wife Abigail:

JOHN ADAMS: September 17, 1774. This is one of the happiest days of my life. In Congress we had generous, noble sentiments, and manly eloquence. This day convinced me that America will support Massachusetts or perish with her.

NARRATOR: Relations between England and America grew worse with the boycott in effect. In the colonies lines were drawn between those who upheld the boycott and those who continued to buy British goods. A man was either a patriot, true to the spirit of America; or he was a Tory, loyal to England. There was no middle ground. And then in April, 1775, a shot was fired that was heard 'round the world. Blood was shed at Lexington and Concord!

VOICE: Disperse, you rebels—damn you, throw down your arms and disperse. (*Sound of shot*)

NARRATOR: Which side fired that first shot is still a mystery. But the die was cast. The Revolutionary War was on. Within a month after Lexington, the Second Continental Congress met in Philadelphia and drew up a fervid statement of the grievances of the colonists . . .

READER: Journals of Congress, Philadelphia. "In brief, we are reduced to the alternative of choosing an unconditional Submission to the tyranny of irritated Ministers, or resistance by Force. The latter is our choice. We have counted the cost of this contest, and find nothing so dreadful as voluntary Slavery. Honour, Justice, and

Humanity, forbid us tamely to surrender that freedom which we received from our gallant Ancestors, and which our innocent Posterity have a right to receive from us."

NARRATOR: The Congress humbly petitioned the King for a redress of wrongs. But its petitions were met with scorn and contempt. Parliament proceeded to raise a great army, including hired Hessian soldiers from Germany, to put down rebellion in the colonies. Shortly, Thomas Paine, who emigrated to America in the midst of the excitement of the year before, wrote a pamphlet called "Common Sense." Over 100,000 copies were distributed in three months and men and women talked about it up and down the Atlantic seaboard.

WOMAN: Thomas Paine doesn't mince words. He calls anything but independence an outrage to common sense.

2ND WOMAN: Isn't that part exciting where he says, "O! ye that love mankind! Ye that dare oppose, not only tyranny, but the tyrant, stand forth! We have it in our power to begin the world over again."

MAN: I wasn't sure before, but Tom Paine makes me see that independence is our only way out.

NARRATOR: John Adams sent a copy of "Common Sense" to Abigail, who greeted it with enthusiasm. General Washington called Paine's arguments unanswerable. He agreed that "an open and determined declaration for independence" was the only solution for America. Thousands of colonists, heretofore wavering, came over to the patriot side, stirred by Paine's ringing words:

READER:

"From the east to the west, blow the trumpet to arms,

Thro' the land let the sound of it flee,
Let the far and the near—all unite with a cheer,
In defence of our Liberty tree."

NARRATOR: In June of 1776 a delegate to Congress from Virginia offered a resolution that "These United States are, and of right ought to be free and independent states." John Adams seconded the resolution. A committee was appointed to draw up a formal declaration of independence, and the actual writing fell to Thomas Jefferson. On the 4th day of July, Congress adopted the momentous Declaration!

READER: "When in the course of human events it becomes necessary for one people to dissolve the political bands which have connected them with another . . . decent respect to the opinions of mankind requires that they should declare the causes which impel them to the separation . . ."

NARRATOR: There followed the deathless preamble and a long list of grievances against the King. And then the resolution . . .

READER: "We, therefore, the Representatives of the United States of America . . . solemnly publish and declare, That these United Colonies are and of Right ought to be *Free and Independent States.*"

NARRATOR: Not all the delegates to the Second Continental Congress were willing to vote for independence. Some felt that the Declaration was premature. After the adjournment of Congress on that memorable day, Benjamin Franklin and John Dickinson stand talking on one side of the room. Both are delegates from Pennsylvania.

FRANKLIN: I hoped until the last, Mr. Dickinson, that you

might change your mind and vote with the majority in our delegation.

DICKINSON: I could not vote against my conscience, sir. I believe the declaration of our independence should have been delayed a while longer.

FRANKLIN: How long, Mr. Dickinson? The King and Parliament will never give in!

DICKINSON: But, Mr. Franklin, we have no army worthy of the name, no way of financing a war against the strongest power in the world.

FRANKLIN: We must depend on help from abroad, and independence is a necessary step in getting it. Now we can obtain a treaty with France . . .

DICKINSON: How can we expect France to unite with us when we have not united with each other? No! Union should come first and then the declaration. I feel we have made ourselves ridiculous in the eyes of foreign powers.

FRANKLIN: Nonsense. But it is a comfort to know that we live in a country where thinking men can differ about the best means to achieve the end we all seek.

NARRATOR: At the very time when Congress was passing the Declaration of Independence, General Washington, in New York, was issuing an order to his troops:

WASHINGTON: The time is now near which must determine whether Americans are to be Freemen or Slaves . . . whether their houses and farms are to be pillaged and destroyed. The fate of unknown millions will now depend, under God, on the courage and conduct of this Army. We have, therefore, to resolve to conquer or die.

NARRATOR: Right at this time the British fleet was sighted off the New Jersey coast. Washington sent word of it to

Congress, the messenger arriving in the midst of the debate.

And how was the Declaration of Independence received by Americans of 1776? The very night it was adopted, John Dunlap, owner of a print shop in Philadelphia, stayed up all night trying to get the stirring words into print by morning. He speaks to his helper as they pick out letters from the type-cases.

DUNLAP: "All men are created equal." Mark what I say . . . there will be volumes spoken and written about those five words.

HELPER: What does it mean? Created equal! You and me equal, Mr. Dunlap? I wouldn't be one to say it myself.

DUNLAP: Equal in the eyes of the Creator, that's what it means. And so all men should be *treated* equal. That's it. Treated alike, and have the same chance.

HELPER: I can say Amen to a thought like that, sir.

DUNLAP: It's what we're going to stand for even more from now on. And the minute we forget, that minute we'll see our liberty beginning to slip through our fingers.

NARRATOR: Dunlap's handbills were on the streets of Philadelphia soon after sun-up. Avidly the citizens of Penn's city read the words. Some men and women were jubilant, some doubtful, some downright angry. But few realized that here, on a page of print, were historic words that would take their place beside the Magna Carta, that first great document to define the rights of man.

In her home near Boston, Abigail Adams received an enthusiastic letter from her delegate-husband. Their 9-year-old son, John Quincy Adams, listens eagerly as she reads the letter aloud:

ABIGAIL: "This will be the most memorable epoch in the history of America. I believe it will be celebrated by succeeding generations as the great anniversary Festival. . . . It ought to be solemnized with Pomp and Parade . . ."

JOHN: Do you think there will be a parade, Mother? In Boston?

ABIGAIL: In all the cities of America, I should think, Johnny. Now listen to the rest of what your father has to say. "It ought to be solemnized with Pomp and Parade, with Shews, Sports, Guns, Bells, Bonfires and Illuminations . . ."

JOHN: Oh, Mother! Bonfires and Illuminations!

ABIGAIL: ". . . from one end of this Continent to the other, from this time forward, forevermore."

JOHN: Every year? An independence celebration every year?

ABIGAIL: That's what your father thinks, and rightly so, for such a tremendous thing as freedom, Johnny. Let's see, there's more. (*Reading voice*) "I am well aware of the Toil and Blood and Treasure it will cost us to maintain this Declaration, and support and defend these states. Yet, through the gloom I can see the rays of light and glory."

JOHN: Do you think a *hundred* years from now, they will still be celebrating, Mother?

ABIGAIL: A hundred years, yes. And two hundred years. And longer. Maybe you can help some time, Johnny, to keep those rays of light and glory shining bright.

NARRATOR: The first big public Fourth of July celebration took place in Philadelphia on July 8th, in that momentous year of 1776. Bells rang all day and most of the night, the Liberty Bell among them, clanging away in the tower of the State House where the Declaration was adopted. Cheering and more cheering resounded through the city. Battalions of soldiers paraded on the Common and fired their guns with unrestrained joy. Even the scarcity of gunpowder did not stand in the way. (*Sound of voices, cheering.*)

VOICES: Three cheers for the United States of America!

OTHER VOICES: Hurrah! Hurrah! Hurrah!

VOICE: Three cheers for freedom and independence!

NARRATOR: It was not until the next day, July 9th, that New York had its big celebration. The Continental army was in camp there, and General Washington had the troops drawn up on parade, to listen to a reading of the Declaration. The soldiers listened in silence to the Preamble and to the long list of abuses charged against the King. Then came the solemn pledge at the end:

READER: "And for the support of this Declaration, with a firm reliance on the protection of Divine Providence, we mutually pledge to each other our Lives, our Fortunes and our sacred Honour."

SOLDIERS (*Voices up*): . . . "we mutually pledge to each other our Lives, our Fortunes and our sacred Honour." (*Great cheers and hurrahs*)

NARRATOR: Other patriots were celebrating on Bowling Green in New York City, where a statue of King George the Third had held the place of honor for six years. The King, robed like a Roman emperor, was seated on a horse. Horse and rider, larger than life, had been cast in lead and covered with gold leaf. The high ironwork fence around the statue could not keep out some of the Sons of Liberty who were bent on destroying the statue of the King.

1ST: Lynch him! Lynch him!

2ND: Topple him over. Here, throw me that rope.

3RD: We'd do better without these fifteen feet of pedestal! Sling a rope around his neck, someone.

1ST: Four thousand pounds—that's what they say the King and his horse weigh. Good British lead. We'll melt it down for bullets.

2ND: Bullets! Thousands of bullets. Tens of thousands. Heave, boys, heave!

3RD: Look out! Here it comes! (*Great crash and cheering*)

4TH: Cut off his head, the rascal! We've no use for a King now we're free and independent states.

NARRATOR: Great bonfires burned in many other cities. Soldiers fired thirteen volleys for the thirteen states, and in the taverns men drank thirteen toasts to the United States of America. In a few days express riders had carried handbills to the newspapers up and down the coast. But news did not reach some of the outlying corners of the States until August, even September.

In the Waxhaw Indian country of South Carolina a group of patriots gathered to hear the first reading of the Declaration in August, 1776. The reader was a 9-year-old boy named Andrew Jackson. He later became the seventh President of the United States. As the meeting breaks up, Andrew's mother and older brother congratulate him.

MRS. JACKSON: You read it real well, Andy. Good and loud so we didn't miss a word.

HUGH: Didn't even stumble over the big words. Unalienable rights! You know what it means?

ANDREW: I asked the preacher. Means rights that can't be given away or taken away. Rights that are ours for keeps.

MRS. JACKSON: I only wish your father could have lived to

see this day, the Lord bless him. Would have been a great day for him, listening to his son reading out the Declaration of Independence.

ANDREW: Pa was always for liberty, wasn't he?

MRS. JACKSON: That he was. 'Twould have delighted his heart, Andy, to hear those words about government being for the safety and happiness of the people, and getting its powers from the people.

HUGH: People like us. Ma, I've decided I'm going to join up and fight. That's something worth fighting for.

MRS. JACKSON: I'd fight for a government of the people myself, if they'd let me.

ANDREW: So would I, if nine years old weren't too young. But I'll fight for freedom *some* day, somehow.

NARRATOR: Well, there it is . . . the story of the noblest document in our whole history, the Declaration of Independence.

The idea of liberty is now ingrained in every American. We take it for granted, just as we take the free union of our forty-eight states for granted. How many of us ever stop to ask what it is that has held our union together for so many years? How many of us ever try to answer that question? Abraham Lincoln did, a hundred years ago . . .

LINCOLN: It was not the mere matter of separation of the colonies from the motherland, but that sentiment in the Declaration of Independence which gave liberty, not alone to the people of this country, but hope to the world, for all future time. It was that which gave promise that in due time the weight would be lifted from the shoulders of all men and that all should have an equal chance.

NARRATOR: That is the secret of the nobility of the Declaration—the promise in it, the promise of liberty not only for the thirteen states along the Atlantic seaboard, but in due time for all men everywhere. Our fore-fathers lived for that promise and died for it. We owe our liberty to them and are grateful for their sacrifice. But now more than gratitude is called for. The tyranny of dictatorship threatens to sweep liberty off the face of the earth and establish in its place a universal police state. The challenge that faces us demands a rededication to the great cause of freedom. In the spirit of '76 we must be willing to live and die that the hope of liberty may be kept alive for all men everywhere.

VOICES: And for the support of this Declaration, we mutually pledge to each other our Lives, our Fortunes and our sacred Honour!

THE END

A Star for Old Glory

(As it might have happened)

Characters

BETSY ROSS
SALLY ⎫
ANN ⎬ *children next door*
JANE ⎭
UNCLE GEORGE ROSS
1ST COMMITTEEMAN
2ND COMMITTEEMAN

TIME: *Afternoon of June 16, 1777.*
SETTING: *The Ross upholstery shop on Arch Street in Philadelphia.*
AT RISE: BETSY ROSS, *a vivacious young woman, works over an easy-chair, fastening down the stuffing.* SALLY *sticks her head in outside door.*

SALLY: Are you busy, Mrs. Ross?
BETSY: Quite busy, Sally.
ANN (*Sticking her head in*): Very, *very* busy?
BETSY: Quite very busy. I'm in the midst of fixing this old easy-chair for Uncle George Ross. And I must say the stuffing is very stubborn.
SALLY: He's the uncle who is in the Continental Con-

gress, isn't he? The one who signed the Declaration of Independence?

BETSY: Yes, my husband's famous uncle—Uncle George. I promised the chair would be ready by Wednesday.

JANE (*Sticking her head in*): But it's only Monday, Mrs. Ross. Monday, June 16, 1777.

BETSY: I know. But I have other things to finish besides Uncle George's chair. Since my husband died and left me to run the shop all by myself, I never get caught up. Seems everyone is having chairs reupholstered these days instead of buying new ones . . . with the War on, and no more chairs coming from England, and prices so high and all.

SALLY: That's why we want to make the doily, Mrs. Ross.

BETSY: Doily?

ANN: For Mamma's birthday.

JANE: Because we haven't any money to buy one.

BETSY: Your projects are always so much more interesting than twine and stuffing! What kind of doily?

SALLY: We'll come back some other time, Mrs. Ross, when you aren't so busy.

JANE: Are you *ever* not so busy?

BETSY: Don't go! Come in and sit down. I'm never too busy to talk to my neighbors. Really, I'm not. I can keep right on working.

SALLY (*Laughing*): That's what you always say.

ANN: But you always don't, Mrs. Ross.

JANE: You start to help us and then forget all about the old twine and stuffing!

BETSY: I know. (*Laughs*) But it's so much more fun to make patterns for samplers and doll clothes—and doilies. (*Gives the chair seat a good poke*) What's that you have behind your back, Ann?

SALLY: I think we'd better not show you—for the sake of Uncle George Ross's chair.

BETSY: Come on, show me. The chair won't run away.

ANN (*Holding up pattern of a large, very lopsided, star*): Can you guess?

BETSY (*Cocking her head*): It has very long ears. Or are they legs? Or both? Perhaps two ears, two legs, and a nose.

GIRLS (*Giggling*): It's a *star*, Mrs. Ross.

BETSY: Heavens to Betsy! You don't say.

SALLY: It's the best we could do.

ANN: We thought a star would be a nice shape for a new doily on Mamma's round table. We'll embroider it with fancy stitches.

JANE: If we can make it look like a star.

BETSY: What a lovely idea! A star-shape for a doily. (*Gets up from work, takes star*) Here, let me see what's wrong with your pattern.

SALLY: There must be some way to make a star so it doesn't look like a lopsided dog!

BETSY: I used to cut out stars when I was young. I was very good at it. But now I'm so old, I wonder if I can remember.

ANN: Are you so *very* old, Mrs. Ross?

BETSY: Oh, dear, yes. Twenty-five. Practically twenty-five and a half.

JANE: That *is* old, isn't it? But maybe you can remember if you think real hard.

BETSY (*Picking up piece of paper and scissors*): Let's see. A star. Hmmmm. There's a certain way to fold the paper, but I'm not sure any more. There's another way, too. I used to cut two triangles, the same length on each side. (*Folds paper, cuts two triangles at same time*).

There. You see, two equal-sided triangles. Now put one over the other, like this, so the points stick out, and what do you have?

GIRLS (*Awed*): A six-pointed star.

JANE: And all the points are the same size.

ANN: You aren't so very old, after all, Mrs. Ross—to remember all that. May we use the pattern for our doily?

BETSY: Of course.

JANE (*Hesitating*): But, look . . . there are only five of us in the family: Mamma, Papa, and we three girls. If it could be a *five*-pointed star, instead of a six-pointed one, then one point would stand for each of us. A six-pointed star doesn't stand for anything.

BETSY: There's something to what you say, Jane.

SALLY: Do you know how to make a five-pointed star, Mrs. Ross? A nice even one like that?

BETSY: There's a way to fold the paper. But I haven't needed to make stars for such a long time. . . . (*Takes paper and folds*)

ANN: I hope you can remember, even if you are so old.

BETSY: Let's see if I can figure out the folds. (*Girls watch intently*.) If we make a five-pointed star by a roundabout method first, then we can fold the paper into the proper creases and know how to do it next time. Triangles won't do this time. We'll need arrowheads, as I remember. Two pointed heads with forked tails, like this (*Snips paper*) Now put them over each other so the tail-points overlap at one place.

GIRLS: Oh!

BETSY: You see, five points. (*Still experimenting*) Now I see how to fold the paper. Four times, and snip!

SALLY: A beautiful five-pointed star. It's much prettier

than the six-pointed one, isn't it? Because the points aren't so squatty.

ANN: I bet you aren't as old as you think you are, Mrs. Ross!

JANE: May we have the pattern? It will make a lovely doily. (*Sound of hoof beats on the cobblestones outside.* SALLY *hurries to look out the window.*)

SALLY: Oh, an elegant coach is stopping in front of the shop. Drawn by four dapple-gray horses.

BETSY: In front of the shop?

SALLY: Right in front.

BETSY: Heavens! With me in the middle of the floor. (*Gets up hurriedly*) I wonder who it can be. (*Looks out window cautiously*) Why, it's Uncle George Ross. And I'm not nearly finished with his chair.

ANN (*Looking*): Another gentleman is getting out, too.

JANE: And another!

BETSY: Dear me. Pick up all the scraps, girls—and hurry! Then slip out the back door. (*Handing pattern to her*) Here, here's your pattern.

(*Flustered,* BETSY *fixes her hair, then turns to work on the chair. Girls gather up scraps and run out back door. In a moment* UNCLE GEORGE *and two other men come in the open door of the shop.*)

UNCLE: Good afternoon, Elizabeth.

BETSY: Why, Uncle George. I'm so sorry, the chair isn't finished yet.

UNCLE: I haven't come to see about the chair, Elizabeth. (*Turns to men*) Gentlemen, this is my niece, Elizabeth Griscom Ross. Her father helped build the State House here in Philadelphia, where Congress has been meeting. Elizabeth, these gentlemen are members of a Congressional Committee.

BETSY: A Congressional Committee! Do be seated, gentle-men. Please excuse the looks of my workroom. When I have everything to tend to myself, I'm afraid . . .

UNCLE: As Chairman of the Committee, niece, it occurred to me you might be a good person to consult, consider-ing your years of experience with needle and thread.

BETSY: Yes, Uncle George?

UNCLE: Have you ever made a flag?

BETSY: No, I don't believe I ever have.

UNCLE: Do you think you could?

BETSY: Make a flag? I don't see why not, Uncle George. It shouldn't be too difficult. Depending on the flag, of course.

UNCLE: Congress finally got around to adopting a design for a national flag two days ago, on the 14th. And I say it's about time.

1ST COMMITTEEMAN: Long overdue!

UNCLE: We can't have every state flying a flag of its own, when we are all united to fight in this war. We can't have Massachusetts hoisting a flag with a pine tree, and South Carolina one with a rattlesnake, and New York one with a beaver, and Rhode Island one with a blue anchor.

2ND COMMITTEEMAN: It's ridiculous.

BETSY: But I thought there was a Continental Flag, one for all the states, Uncle George. Haven't I seen it dozens of times? The flag with thirteen red and white stripes and the British Union Jack in the corner, with the crosses of St. George and St. Andrew?

UNCLE: That flag makes me hot under the collar every time I see it. Yes, Elizabeth, we have been flying that flag since the beginning of 1776, and I say it's ridicu-lous. The Union Jack indeed!

2ND COMMITTEEMAN: It was all right to include the British symbol when we were still colonies and felt loyalty to the Crown. But since our Declaration of Independence that flag has been out of place, to say the least.

1ST COMMITTEEMAN: We need a flag of our own. A flag of independence!

UNCLE: Last Saturday, Congress finally got around to adopting a flag resolution, Elizabeth. (*Takes slip of paper from pocket and reads*) "Resolved that the flag of the United States shall be thirteen stripes, alternate red and white, with a union of thirteen stars of white on a blue field, representing a new constellation."

BETSY: A new constellation—a group of stars standing for our new country!

1ST COMMITTEEMAN: One for each state.

UNCLE: Here, Elizabeth, is a rough design of the plan. You see the thirteen stripes, and here in the corner, thirteen stars on a blue field. It has been suggested the stars be arranged in a circle.

BETSY: The design shows six-pointed stars.

UNCLE: Yes, they look a bit squat, don't they? But they are so much easier to make.

BETSY: A five-pointed star is much more interesting, gentlemen. With longer points . . .

1ST COMMITTEEMAN: But how can a five-pointed star be made, except with the greatest difficulty?

BETSY: Look. It's not difficult at all. I used to make them when I was a child. (*Takes paper, folds it four times, snips and holds up a five-pointed star, like the pattern for the girls. Note: Pattern can be all arranged beforehand if desired.*)

UNCLE: Amazing! A perfect star. I was sure you would be the one to consult, Elizabeth.

2ND COMMITTEEMAN: Unbelievable! A perfect five-pointed star.

UNCLE: By all means make up the flag with five-pointed stars. Don't you agree, gentlemen?

1ST COMMITTEEMAN: Yes, yes.

UNCLE: And will you be able to make it soon? I think it a disgrace to use the old Continental flag one day longer than necessary. (*Sees* BETSY *looking at his unfinished chair*) There's no hurry about my chair, Elizabeth. No hurry at all.

BETSY: No? Then I can start on the flag immediately.

UNCLE: Good!

2ND COMMITTEEMAN: Excellent.

UNCLE: A flag of our own. With thirteen stars representing a new constellation—a brilliant new constellation. I am sure that is not too much to say of the United States of America. Well, Elizabeth . . .

BETSY: I shall let you know as soon as I finish the flag, Uncle George. Thank you, gentlemen. I can't tell you what a privilege this is to work on the new flag. What a wonderful change from—(*Looks at* UNCLE GEORGE'S *unfinished chair*)—from stuffing. Good day to you all.

COMMITTEEMEN (*Leaving*): Good day, Mrs. Ross.

UNCLE: Good day, Elizabeth. (*They go out.*) (BETSY *stands happily looking at the rough sketch.* SALLY *sticks her head in back door.*)

SALLY: Are you busy, Mrs. Ross?

BETSY: I think I shall be quite busy for a little while, Sally.

ANN (*Sticking her head in*): Are you *always* busy, Mrs. Ross? Cutting out stars?

JANE: Five-pointed stars!

BETSY: Have you been listening?

JANE: We couldn't help it. We wanted to ask you something else—about a larger pattern.

SALLY: We heard all about the new flag and everything.

BETSY: Come in, girls. Sit down. Thanks to you, I still remember how to cut five-pointed stars. Snip! Snip! The gentlemen were amazed.

GIRLS: Weren't they, though.

JANE: Now you'll be busier than ever, won't you? Making a brand new flag.

SALLY: We don't like to bother you, Mrs. Ross. . . .

BETSY: Bother me! Why, girls, I'm just thanking my *stars* that I have such helpful neighbors!

THE END

Sing, America, Sing

(An American heritage pageant with music)

Characters

(Many parts may be doubled up)

NARRATOR
GIRLS CHORUS
STAGEHAND
TWO WOMEN
SONS OF LIBERTY
RAGGED CONTINENTALS
FRANCIS SCOTT KEY
JOHN SKINNER
SAILORS
LUMBERJACKS
MULE DRIVER
COTTON PICKERS
TWO RAILWAY WORKERS
UNION SOLDIERS
CONFEDERATE SOLDIERS
DANIEL, JAMIE *and* REBECCA BOONE
PIONEERS
COWBOYS

World War Soldiers
Radio Voice

Note: Words and music for the well-known songs in this play may be obtained from many different song books. The less familiar songs marked with an asterisk (*) may be found in *A Treasury of American Song,* by Downes and Siegmeister, published by Alfred A. Knopf, New York.

Setting: *Large, bare stage.*

At Rise: Narrator *stands at one side.* Girls Chorus, *which will be on stage throughout the play, stands or sits at back. As curtain opens* Chorus *is softly singing 1st stanza of "America the Beautiful."*

Narrator: Sing, America, sing! Sing of the past and the present, of peace and war. Sing of the beginnings and endings and goings-on. Sing of the days when we were thirteen colonies along the Atlantic seaboard, in a new world, facing a new horizon. Thirteen states waiting for a new flag!

Chorus (*Speaking in turn, staccato*): New Hampshire . . . Massachusetts . . . Rhode Island . . . Connecticut . . . New York . . . New Jersey . . . Delaware . . . Pennsylvania . . . Maryland . . . Virginia . . . North Carolina . . . South Carolina . . . Georgia.

Narrator: Sing of a word called *liberty* beginning to stir through the colonies like a breeze off the sea, gathering strength, gathering force, sweeping along the coast . . . shipyard to crossroad, crossroad to farmhouse, farmhouse to tavern, tavern to cobblestone street.

Chorus (*Softly at first, mounting to fortissimo*): Liberty . . . liberty . . . liberty . . . liberty . . . LIBERTY. (Stagehand *enters on side opposite* Narrator, *puts up*

sign reading NEW YORK, 1769. *Exits.* Two Women
enter, talking.)

1st Woman: It's always exciting to walk past the Common and see if the Liberty Pole is still standing. *(Stops,
looks, points)* Look, the banner still flaps defiance at
the British soldiers.

2nd Woman *(Nodding)*: So that is your Liberty Pole! I've
heard about it, even in Boston. A sacred symbol in the
struggle against tyranny. No taxation without representation!

1st Woman: I should say not. We won't stand for it. Our
Sons of Liberty in New York guard the Pole like bull-
dogs. Three times the British have cut it down. Four
times the Sons of Liberty have raised it! This fourth
Pole has survived for several years now.

2nd Woman: How could the British cut it down—with
those iron bars around it, held in place by metal hoops!

1st Woman: They have tried. Not only to cut it down,
but to undermine it and blow it up. And each time
they failed.

2nd Woman: And if they do manage to destroy it, your
Sons of Liberty will raise another. *(Cocks ear)* Listen!

1st Woman *(Listening, as strains of music are heard offstage, voices singing)*: The Liberty Song!* Everyone is
singing it here . . . that is, everyone on our side.

2nd Woman: We sing it in Boston, too. *(They step back
to join* Chorus *as* Sons of Liberty *come in singing.*)

Sons of Liberty:

Come join hand in hand, brave Americans all,
And rouse your bold hearts at fair Liberty's call;
No tyrannous acts shall suppress your just claim,
Or stain with dishonour America's name.

CHORUS (*Joins in*):
 In Freedom we're born and in Freedom we'll live,
 Our purses are ready,
 Steady, Friends, Steady,
 Not as Slaves, but as Free men our money we'll give.
(SONS OF LIBERTY *pass hats*; CHORUS *and* WOMEN *put in coins.* SONS OF LIBERTY *sing again.*)
SONS OF LIBERTY:
 Then join hand in hand, brave Americans all,
 (*They join with* CHORUS *and* WOMEN *and circle around stage.*)
    By uniting we stand, by dividing we fall;
    In so righteous a cause let us hope to succeed,
    For Heaven approves of each generous deed.
 (*They break circle, and* SONS OF LIBERTY *pass hats again as they all swing into the chorus of "The Liberty Song." On last line,* SONS OF LIBERTY *march out;* CHORUS *moves back in place;* TWO WOMEN *exit.* STAGEHAND *enters, removes sign, and exits.*)
NARRATOR: Sing, America, sing of the long hard war for liberty and independence—1775 to 1783—years of suffering and hardship, doubt and faith, hope and uncertainty. Sing of courage in the face of overwhelming odds.
CHORUS (*Speaking in turn, staccato*): Lexington . . . Concord . . . Bunker Hill . . . Trenton . . . Germantown . . . Valley Forge . . . Monmouth . . . Charleston . . . Camden . . . Yorktown.
NARRATOR: Sing of General Washington and his ragged Continentals! (CONTINENTALS *march in, singing "Yankee Doodle."*)
CONTINENTALS:
        Fath'r and I went down to camp

Along with Captain Good'in,
And there we saw the men and boys
As thick as hasty puddin'.

CHORUS (*Taking over while* CONTINENTALS *mark time.*
CHORUS *might put on paper soldier caps, each with a
big feather*):
Yankee Doodle keep it up,
Yankee Doodle dandy,
Mind the music and the step
And with the girls be handy.

CONTINENTALS:
And there was General Washington
Upon a slapping stallion,
Agiving orders to his men:
I guess there were a million.

CHORUS (*Repeats chorus, as* CONTINENTALS *maneuver and
march out*):
Yankee Doodle keep it up (*Etc.*)

NARRATOR: Sing, America, sing. Sing of the long war over
and independence won. Sing of the blessings of liberty
secured to ourselves and our posterity. Sing of our new
nation stretching and spreading, reaching toward the
west . . . up the river valleys, through the forests, over
the mountains. Sing of new states coming into the
Union.

CHORUS (*In turn*): Vermont . . . Kentucky . . . Tennes-
see . . . Ohio . . . Louisiana. (CHORUS *swings into*
"*Hail, Columbia!*")
Firm, united let us be
Rallying round our Liberty!
As a band of brothers join'd,
Peace and safety we shall find.

NARRATOR: And sing of the War of 1812 that gave Francis Scott Key the idea for our national anthem.

(STAGEHAND *enters, puts up sign:* CHESAPEAKE BAY, SEPT., 1814, *exits.* FRANCIS SCOTT KEY *comes in, paces nervously, peers out, jots down note on envelope.* JOHN SKINNER *enters.*)

SKINNER: Aren't you going to rest at all, Mr. Key? You've been pacing the deck all night, back and forth, back and forth.

KEY: Not all night, Mr. Skinner. Some of the time I have stood silently staring across the Bay at Fort McHenry.

SKINNER: Watching the bombs bursting in air . . .

KEY: Yes, and the rockets' red glare. Through the flashing brightness of the bombardment, I have strained my eyes to see if our flag kept flying.

SKINNER (*Peering out*): And is it still flying?

KEY: The last I saw, yes. Fort McHenry has not surrendered. I wish I might have been there to help defend it, sir, instead of fidgeting out here in the Bay detained by the British fleet.

SKINNER: At least, our rescue mission was a success. The British released the prisoner and we can take him back to Baltimore with us when the siege is lifted. Thank God the British Admiral was wrong about the bombardment, Mr. Key!

KEY: Expecting to capture Fort McHenry in a few hours! Why, they've been shelling the Fort for a day and a night and, if I'm not mistaken, our flag *still* flies over it. (*Peers out*) I wish I could see for sure. (*As* KEY *and* SKINNER *strain their eyes,* CHORUS *sings first stanza of "The Star-Spangled Banner," pantomiming as if they, too, were on deck watching anxiously.*)

CHORUS:

> Oh, say, can you see, by the dawn's early light,
> What so proudly we hailed at the twilight's last gleam-
>   ing?
> Whose broad stripes and bright stars, through the peril-
>   ous fight,
> O'er the ramparts we watched were so gallantly stream-
>   ing!
> And the rockets' red glare, the bombs bursting in air,
> Gave proof through the night that our flag was still
>   there;
> *(Voices up)*
> Oh, say, does that star-spangled banner yet wave
> O'er the land of the free and the home of the brave!

SKINNER: If only we could catch the gleam of the first light of dawn on our flag, Mr. Key!

KEY *(Making note on envelope)*: Catching the gleam of the morning's first beam . . .

SKINNER: You are a poet as well as a lawyer?

KEY: Oh, occasionally I am moved to write verses. All last night, while the bombs were bursting, my brain was on fire. Not just kindled, sir, but on fire . . . as I thought about our star-spangled banner waving bravely through the fight. *(Taps envelope)* I have words here, phrases here, that need only to be put together when I reach Baltimore. They will make a song, perhaps.

CHORUS *(Up suddenly, excited)*:

> Now it catches the gleam of the morning's first beam,
> In full glory reflected now shines on the stream;
> 'Tis the star-spangled banner; oh, long may it wave
> O'er the land of the free and the home of the brave!
> *(KEY and SKINNER exit during the singing. STAGEHAND enters, removes sign, exits.)*

NARRATOR: Sing, America, of white stars on a field of blue, a star for every state, and every state growing, developing. Wagons creaking. Hammers pounding. Sails flapping. Axes ringing. Millstones grinding. Clipper ships sailing the seven seas. Sing of America at work, making our country great! (SAILORS *enter singing "Blow, Boys, Blow." * As they sing, they pantomime pulling on ropes to hoist sails.*)

SOLO: A Yankee ship came down the river,

SAILORS: Blow, boys, blow!

SOLO: Her masts and yards they shone like silver.

SAILORS: Blow, my bully boys, blow!

SOLO: How do you know she's a Yankee liner?

SAILORS: Blow, boys, blow!

SOLO: The Stars and Stripes float out behind her.

SAILORS: Blow, my bully boys, blow! (*One of the* SAILORS *might go into a hornpipe here. Or the* CHORUS *might do a sailor dance if that seems more practicable. Then* SAILORS *take up their song again.*)

SOLO: Blow, boys, blow, the sun's drawing water.

SAILORS: Blow, boys, blow!

SOLO: Three cheers for the cook and one for his daughter.

SAILORS (*Exiting*): Blow, my bully boys, blow!

NARRATOR: Sing of the lumberjack cutting down the white pines in New England forests . . . trimming a tall straight mast . . . sawing logs for timbers and building-boards . . . riding the logs down the river on the spring flood. (*Several* LUMBERJACKS *enter. They swing axes in pantomime as they sing "A Shantyman's Life." **)

LUMBERJACKS:

    Oh a shantyman's life is a wearisome life

    Although some think it void of care.

Swinging an ax from morning till night,
In the midst of the forests so drear.

Lying in the shanty—bleak and cold
While the cold, stormy wintery winds blow,
And as soon as the daylight doth appear,
To the wild woods we must go.

(LUMBERJACKS *repeat last two lines as they go out.*)

NARRATOR: Sing of the mule-drivers pulling boats and barges along the Erie Canal, night and day, day and night—moving passengers and produce and drawing the country together. (MULE DRIVER *enters, pantomiming driving his mule, singing "The Erie Canal." **)

MULE DRIVER: I've got a mule and her name is Sal,
CHORUS: Fifteen miles on the Erie Canal—
MULE DRIVER: She's a good old worker and a good old pal,
CHORUS: Fifteen miles on the Erie Canal.

MULE DRIVER:

We've hauled some barges in our day,
Filled with lumber, coal and hay,
And we know every inch of the way
From Albany to Buffalo.

CHORUS AND DRIVER:

Low bridge, everybody down!

(CHORUS *ducks down*)

For it's Low Bridge, we're coming to a town!

(*Down again*)

You can always tell your neighbor,
You can always tell your pal,
If you've ever navigated on the Erie Canal.

(MULE DRIVER *and* CHORUS *may sing another stanza, "We better get along on our way, old gal," etc., with chorus if desired.* MULE DRIVER *goes out at end of chorus.*)

NARRATOR: Sing of the blacksmith, the miller, the farmer, the storekeeper, the fisherman, the baker, the candlestick maker. Sing of the miner, the tavern keeper, the peddler trekking down the road with a pack on his back. Sing of all the men and women building America, making it strong. And sing in a minor key of the cotton pickers in the South . . . in the days when one human being could own another. (*Three or four girls,* COTTON PICKERS, *come in with sacks in which they pantomime putting cotton as they pick it. They sing "Nobody Knows de Trouble I See.")*

COTTON PICKERS:

> Nobody knows de trouble I see,
> Nobody knows but Jesus;
> Nobody knows de trouble I see,
> Glory hallelujah!

SOLO: Sometimes I'm up, sometimes I'm down,

ALL: Oh, yes, Lord;

SOLO: Sometimes I'm almost to de groun',

ALL: Oh, yes, Lord. (*They move offstage slowly, humming as they pick cotton.*)

NARRATOR: Sing of the husky immigrants working on the railroads, pushing the gleaming rails across the prairies, through the heart of America, into the mountains. (TWO RAILWAY WORKERS *enter. They pantomime driving spikes, taking turns hitting the spike with a sledge hammer. They sing "Pat Works on the Railway." **)

1ST WORKER:

> In eighteen hundred and forty one
> I put me corduroy britches on,
> I put me corduroy britches on
> To work upon the railway.

BOTH:

    Fi-li-me-oo-re-oo-re-ay, (*Etc.*)

2ND WORKER:

    It's "Pat, do this," and "Pat, do that!"
    Without a stocking or a hat,
    And nothing but an old cravat,
    While Pat works on the railway.

BOTH:

    Fi-li-me-oo-re-oo-re-ay, (*Etc.*)

(RAILWAY WORKERS *exit as* CHORUS *sings "She'll Be Comin' Round the Mountain." They shade their eyes, look off stage expectantly, nod at each other, look again.*)

CHORUS: She'll be comin' round the mountain when she comes. (*Etc. If possible the toot of a train whistle should be heard offstage as the song ends.*)

NARRATOR: Sing of America continuing to grow and stretch. Sixteen new white stars added to the field of blue between the War of 1812 and the War between the States! Sixteen new shining stars.

CHORUS (*Speaking in turn, staccato*): Indiana . . . Mississippi . . . Illinois . . . Alabama . . . Maine . . . Missouri . . . Arkansas . . . Michigan . . . Florida . . . Texas . . . Iowa . . . Wisconsin . . . California . . . Minnesota . . . Oregon . . . Kansas.

NARRATOR: And then came the war between the States, on the heels of the great debates over slavery.

1ST IN CHORUS: Abraham Lincoln has been saying for years that this country cannot endure half slave and half free.

2ND: Stephen A. Douglas doesn't agree with him.

3RD: Nobody wants war, but sometimes there seems to be no other way out.

4TH: Lincoln's idea of democracy is that we should neither be slaves nor masters.

5TH: They say in the South that slavery is good for both the whites and the blacks.

6TH: Who says it? Not the Negroes!

NARRATOR: Union soldiers were on the march after the attack on Fort Sumter, and in time "The Battle Hymn of the Republic" became their marching song. (CHORUS *sings first stanza of "The Battle Hymn of the Republic" as* UNION SOLDIERS *march in and drill on left of stage.*)

NARRATOR: And here come Confederate soldiers on the march, to the tune of "Dixie." (CHORUS *sings chorus of "Dixie" as* CONFEDERATE SOLDIERS *march in and stand at right.*)

NARRATOR: And sing of the two forces together, Union and Confederate, both weary for home, wanting the war to stop, dreaming the same dreams, singing the same song . . .

(UNION *and* CONFEDERATE SOLDIERS *move around as if setting up camp, singing "Tenting Tonight."* *)

SOLDIERS (*Softly*):
We're tenting tonight on the old camp ground,
Give us a song to cheer
Our weary hearts, a song of home
And friends we love so dear.

SOLO UNION SOLDIER:
Many are the hearts that are weary tonight,
Wishing for the war to cease;

SOLO CONFED. SOLDIER:
Many are the hearts that are looking for the right,
To see the dawn of peace.

SOLDIERS:
Tenting tonight, tenting tonight,

Tenting on the old camp ground.

NARRATOR: Sing of the war over and the Union safe. The re-united States of America! Sing of soldiers marching not to battle, but home again to the farms and towns of the North and South, to the loved ones left behind. Sing, America, sing! (CHORUS *joyously sings "When Johnny Comes Marching Home,"* * *as* SOLDIERS *begin to march, some offstage, some changing places. This should be a very lively scene.*)

CHORUS: When Johnny comes marching home again,

SOLDIERS: Hurrah! Hurrah!

CHORUS: We'll give him a hearty welcome then,

SOLDIERS: Hurrah! Hurrah!

CHORUS: The men will cheer, the boys will shout, (*Etc.*) (CHORUS *goes into second stanza, "The old church bell will peal with joy," and* SOLDIERS *again take the "Hurrahs!" During chorus,* SOLDIERS *begin to leave stage.*)

NARRATOR: Sing, America—sing of the pioneers forever searching for the promised land. Sing of the fearless, self-reliant men and women who kept pushing the frontier farther and farther west . . . : building their cabins, tilling their piece of good earth, helping to make our country big and broad, beginning even before the Revolution. (CHORUS *might put on sunbonnets for this section. They keep swinging into the refrain from "The Promised Land"* * *as a sort of undertone for the scene.*

CHORUS:

> I am bound for the promised land,
> I'm bound for the promised land,
> Oh, who will come and go with me?
> I am bound for the promised land.

NARRATOR: Sing of pioneers pressing westward on foot,

on horseback, in covered wagon . . . taming the wilderness, turning prairies into cornfields. Sing of Daniel Boone and the thousands and hundreds of thousands who came after him, lured by the adventure of pushing our frontiers westward. (STAGEHAND *enters and puts out placard*—BOONE'S FARM, NORTH CAROLINA, 1769. *He exits.* DANIEL BOONE *and son,* JAMIE, *enter.*)

JAMIE: What's beyond the hills, Pappy?

DANIEL: Sights. Wondrous sights.

JAMIE: What's beyond the mountains?

DANIEL: More sights. (*Points*) Beyond this here state there's Tennessee and Kentucky-land. Wilderness country. Like paradise, Jamie.

JAMIE: Heard you talking to that Finley man yesterday, Pappy. (REBECCA BOONE *comes in behind them, stands listening.*)

DANIEL: He's off to explore Kentucky, Finley is. And I've an itching in my feet to go along. If it weren't for your mother, now, and the younger children . . .

REBECCA: You don't have to be worryin' about us, Dan'l. (DANIEL *and* JAMIE *turn with a start.*) Weather's good, now spring is here. We'll be all right this summer. Might be you could find us a good home site in Kentucky, Dan'l.

DANIEL (*Excited*): It sounds like the promised land to me, Rebecca. Wouldn't be a-tall surprised if I could find the best home site we ever laid eyes on! (*As they go out,* CHORUS *sings, "I am bound for the promised land," etc.* STAGEHAND *enters, removes sign, exits.*)

NARRATOR: Sing of thousands and hundreds of thousands fired by the spirit of Daniel Boone. (TWO WOMEN *enter.*)

1st Woman: Amos was talkin' to Ebèn Smith. He's just back from a trip to El-a-noy. Come to get his folks.

2nd Woman: El-a-noy? Where's that?

1st Woman: Over past Indiana. Not a bad trip, Amos says. And the soil! He never saw such soil! He's tellin' everyone. Reckon half the county will be movin' out. We're goin', Amos and me. (*As the* Women *exit, a group of* Pioneers *come in singing "El-a-noy."* *)

Pioneers:

Way down upon the Wabash,

Sich land was never known, (*Etc.*)

(*As* Pioneers *finish song, they should go into a lively square dance. Or, if this does not seem practicable, one of the* Pioneers *might strum "Oh Susanna!" on the guitar. As the* Pioneers *exit,* Chorus *again repeats "I am bound for the promised land."*)

Narrator: Sing of pioneers discovering gold in California in 1849, and in the Rocky Mountains ten years later. Sing of picks and shovels and tin pans scraping the creek bottoms . . . and wild eyes and fevered brows. Sing of fortunes made and fortunes lost, and America amazing the world with the abundance of her resources. Sing of more and more stars added to the flag as the west was opened up.

Chorus: West Virginia . . . Nevada . . . Nebraska . . . Colorado.

Narrator: The country was filling up, the homesteads were being taken. Where millions of buffalo had roamed a few years before, cows grazed in green pastures. Where buffalo grass had curled rich and sweet over the prairie, corn and wheat were growing. Our country was a flower unfolding—an American beauty rose. (Chorus *sings stanza of "America the Beautiful."*)

NARRATOR: Sing, America, of whistles . . . (*Sound of various whistles offstage, if possible.*)

NARRATOR: Factory whistles, mine whistles, mill whistles, train whistles. And sing of wheels—spinning wheels, wagon wheels, paddlewheels, wheels of engines and locomotives. And sing, America, of hoofs . . . the hoofs of cows and oxen, and horses and mules. Sing of the mustang horses driven up the Chisholm Trail and the millions of longhorn cattle. (COWBOYS *come in twirling ropes, singing "The Chisholm Trail."* *)

SOLO COWBOY:
Well, come along boys and listen to my tale,
I'll tell you of my troubles on the Old Chisholm Trail.

COWBOYS: Coma ti yi youpy, (*Etc.*)

2ND SOLO COWBOY:
Oh! it's bacon and beans 'most every day,
I'd as soon be a-eatin' prairie hay.

COWBOYS: Coma ti yi youpy, (*Etc.*)

3RD SOLO COWBOY:
I went up to the boss to draw my roll,
He had it figgered out I was nine dollars in the hole.

COWBOYS: Coma ti yi youpy, (*Etc.*)

4TH SOLO:
My seat is in the saddle and my saddle's in the sky,
An' I'll quit punchin' cows in the sweet bye and bye.

COWBOYS: Coma ti yi youpy, (*Etc.*) (*As they go out twirling their ropes,* CHORUS *sings "Good-bye, Old Paint."* *)

CHORUS: Good-bye, old Paint, I'm a-leavin' Cheyenne, (*Etc.*)

NARRATOR: In just two years, 1889 and 1890, six new states came into the Union:

CHORUS: North Dakota . . . South Dakota . . . Montana . . . Washington . . . Idaho . . . Wyoming.

NARRATOR: And sing of the last three states to complete the United States of America—Oklahoma, New Mexico and Arizona. By 1912, our flag that started with thirteen stars had forty-eight. Forty-eight stars on a field of blue next to thirteen stripes of red and white.

CHORUS (*Speaking*):
> Red for courage to do the right,
> White for faith with its guiding light,
> Blue for strength in carrying-through—
> Hail to the red and white and blue!

NARRATOR: And then came another war, the first World War . . . and we were there, hoping to make the world safe for democracy—the kind of democracy we had and cherished. Our men were on the march again, in a strange land this time, with unfamiliar names.

CHORUS (*Staccato*): The Somme . . . Verdun . . . Caporetto . . . the Aisne . . . the Meuse-Argonne.

NARRATOR: Our men were on the march. (SOLDIERS *come in marching, single file, a continuous line across stage, as* CHORUS *sings, "Over There."*)

CHORUS (*At end of song, staccato*): Knit . . . make bandages . . . mail packages . . . write letters . . . keep the home fires burning . . . and pray!

NARRATOR: Sing, America, of November 11, 1918, the Armistice signed, and our boys on their way back home. (CHORUS *puts on an Armistice Day demonstration, waving flags, shouting, tooting horns, making a great deal of noise.* SOLDIERS *come marching back singing "Hinky Dinky." ** *)

NARRATOR: Sing, America, of peace again, and our country moving ahead. Automobiles on the highways. Radios in the living rooms. And chicken every Sunday. Sing of the age of the common man, the workingman coming into his own. And then another war, World War II, so close on the heels of the last! (SOLDIERS *cross stage again, this time singing "Praise the Lord and Pass the Ammunition.")*

CHORUS: Pearl Harbor . . . Bataan . . . Corregidor . . . Guadalcanal . . . the Aleutians . . . the Battle of the Bulge . . . the atom bomb! (STAGEHAND *enters with sign:* ANY TOWN, U.S.A., AUG. 6, 1945. *He exits as* RADIO VOICE *comes over loudspeaker.)*

RADIO VOICE: This morning the first atom bomb in history was dropped on Hiroshima, Japan! It will be impossible to tell the extent of the destruction for days . . . possibly months. Scientists estimate that at least half the population of the city and more than half the buildings have been destroyed. Dropped from an American plane, the bomb came as a complete surprise. What the effect of this new weapon of warfare will be, no one can say at this moment. (RADIO VOICE *off, as* TWO WOMEN *enter.)*

1ST WOMAN: I don't like it.

2ND WOMAN: It was the quickest way to end the war, Elizabeth. Japan can't hold out now.

1ST WOMAN: But I don't believe man should have such power in his hands.

2ND WOMAN: Well, he has it.

1ST WOMAN: There's only a one-way street ahead for us now. We've got to use the atom for *peace,* not war. For building-up, not tearing down. It's the world's only salvation.

2ND WOMAN: Atoms for peace—that's not a bad idea. But . . .

1ST WOMAN: There can't be any "but." It's civilization's only hope. That, and the UN. Let me tell you, the days of the pioneer aren't over. We have new frontiers to conquer—glorious frontiers.

2ND WOMAN: What do you mean, Elizabeth?

1ST WOMAN: The frontiers of a new age . . . the atomic age that lies ahead, just around the corner. We can make this world a better world than it has ever been before. (*The* TWO WOMEN *go out;* STAGEHAND *enters and removes sign. Exits.*)

NARRATOR: Sing, America, sing with a stout heart of the age that lies ahead, around the corner. Sing of atoms for peace. Sing of our United States as part of the United Nations, helping to make the world a place of peace and safety, a place of plenty and opportunity for everyone. Sing of what free men can do for the cause of freedom. (CHORUS *sings "A New Wind A-Blowin'." **)

CHORUS:

"There's a brand new wind a-blowin' down the Lincoln road.

There's a brand new hope a-growin' where freedom's seeds are sowed," (*Etc.*)

NARRATOR: Sing, America. Sing of the freedom that is ours to cherish. Sing of songs unwritten and of great words said. Sing of the spirit that must never perish. Sing of the road well-traveled, and the road ahead. Sing, America, sing! (SAILORS, PIONEERS, COWBOYS, SOLDIERS, *etc. come back on stage as everyone sings "God Bless America."*)

THE END

Washington Marches On

(A Living Newspaper)

Characters

Scene 1: AUGUSTINE WASHINGTON, *Virginia planter*

Scene 2:
- BETTY WASHINGTON, *13*
- GEORGE WASHINGTON, *14*
- SAMUEL WASHINGTON, *12*
- MARY BALL WASHINGTON, *their mother*

Scene 3:
- LORD FAIRFAX
- LAWRENCE WASHINGTON
- GEORGE WASHINGTON, *almost 16*

Scene 4:
- ANNE FAIRFAX WASHINGTON
- GEORGE WASHINGTON, *20*

Scene 5:
- GENERAL BRADDOCK
- GEORGE WASHINGTON, *23*
- 1ST SOLDIER
- 2ND SOLDIER
- 3RD SOLDIER

Scene 6:
- BETTY WASHINGTON LEWIS, *25*
- MARY BALL WASHINGTON

Scene 7:
- VOICE FROM AUDIENCE
- GEORGE WASHINGTON, *43*
- JOHN ADAMS

53

Scene 8:
- 1ST SENTRY
- 2ND SENTRY
- MESSENGER

Scene 9:
- MARTHA WASHINGTON
- GEORGE WASHINGTON, *46*
- ORDERLY
- MARQUIS DE LAFAYETTE

Scene 10:
- 1ST NEWSBOY
- 2ND NEWSBOY

Scene 11:
- GEORGE WASHINGTON, *52*
- NELLY CUSTIS, *5*

Scene 12:
- CHANCELLOR LIVINGSTON
- GEORGE WASHINGTON, *57*
- VOICES FROM AUDIENCE

Scene 13: SCHOOLMASTER

Scene 14: BOYS *and* GIRLS *with flags.*

CHORUS: *Any number of boys and girls.*

NOTE: *This play may be staged as simply or as elaborately as desired, with or without costumes.* CHORUS *may sit on one side of the stage, or in the audience. If the play is given in front of a classroom, blackboard may be used for dates. Otherwise, large date-cards should be lined up against back wall as play progresses.*

SETTING: *On stage are two chairs and a table holding paper, ink and quill pen. Any scenes requiring furniture take place near these furnishings. All other scenes take place at other parts of the stage.*

CHORUS:

When was he born, George Washington?
What was the place and date?

Solo

(Holding up card or writing on blackboard: Born—1732):

Seventeen hundred thirty-two.
Virginia, the State.

Scene 1

At Rise: Augustine Washington, *a Virginia planter, comes in excitedly, goes to table, takes paper and quill and begins to write.*

Augustine *(As he writes)*: Wakefield on the Potomac
February 22, 1732
To Lawrence and Augustine Washington
Appleby School. England
My Dear Sons: It is with great pleasure that I inform you that you now have a half-brother, born this very day. The baby and his mother are doing well. We have decided, after some discussion, to name him George. Unfortunately it may be some years before you will be able to make his acquaintance.

I trust you are doing well in your studies and working diligently. I trust also that you are enjoying this acquaintance with our mother country. Enclosed you will find a draft of money for your use, over and above expenses, in celebration of the happy event that has taken place today. Your affectionate father, Augustine Washington.

(He nods with satisfaction, seals letter, hurries out with it.)
Chorus: Washington marches on!

*   *   *

Chorus:

How did he grow, George Washington?

SOLO:

Strong as a sturdy tree.

CHORUS:

Did he have hopes and youthful dreams?

SOLO:

(*Holding up card or writing on blackboard: 1746—To Sea?*):

He wanted to go to sea!

SCENE 2

AT RISE: GEORGE, BETTY, *and* SAMUEL *hurry in with packet of mail.*

BETTY: *What* will Uncle Joseph's letter say, I wonder . . . about your going to sea, George? I hope he doesn't say you should.

GEORGE: When I want to go so badly, Betty?

BETTY: But I don't *like* to think of you going so far away. And it's so *dangerous*. That's what Mama says.

SAMUEL: George isn't afraid of danger. Are you, George?

BETTY: I wonder if Uncle Joseph knows how *anxious* we've been waiting to hear from him? (*Takes up letter, tries to look through envelope.*) It certainly takes a long time for a letter to get from London, England, to Fredericksburg, Virginia.

GEORGE: Too long. I've had my things packed for weeks. And Lawrence has the promise of a commission in the Navy for me. All I need is for Mother to say *yes*. (*Sighs*) I wish she'd listen to brother Lawrence, instead of asking Uncle Joseph.

BETTY: She thinks Lawrence is too young to give advice.

SAMUEL: He's twenty-eight. That's old!

GEORGE: And he's married to Anne Fairfax, and he's been in the Navy fighting in the West Indies, and he's master of Mount Vernon, and . . .

BETTY: Still, Mama thinks Uncle Joseph knows best. You know how she has depended on him, ever since Father died.

GEORGE: Well, there's a good chance he'll say yes, anyway. (*Calls*) Mother! Mother! The letter has come from London. From Uncle Joseph.

MRS. WASHINGTON (*Hurrying in excitedly*): The letter! Did I hear you say the letter has come? At last. (*She takes it, hesitates*) I *trust* your Uncle's judgment is the same as mine. (*Opens letter*) Hmmmm. (*Reads to herself while others watch.*)

BETTY: What does he *say*, Mama?

GEORGE (*Anxiously*): May I go?

MRS. WASHINGTON: Listen to this: "I understand that you have some thoughts of putting your son George to sea. I think he had better be put apprentice to a *tinker*. The common sailor has no liberties . . . they will use him like a dog." (*To* GEORGE) Do you hear, George? It is not only dangerous to go to sea, but they'd use you like a dog! So . . . it is decided. After this excellent advice from your Uncle, assuredly you must not go to sea. What else is there in the post, Betty? (*She and* BETTY *exit one side, looking at mail.* GEORGE *and* SAMUEL *start out other side.*)

GEORGE (*Obviously disappointed*): Want to drive stakes for me, Sammy? I suppose there's nothing to do now but practice with Father's surveying instruments. (*Brightens*) There's something like an ocean . . . an endless sea . . . about the wilderness. If I could be a surveyor in the wilderness, I wouldn't mind not going to sea . . . very much. (*They exit.*)

CHORUS: Washington marches on!

* * *

CHORUS:

When did he help survey the lands
that rich Lord Fairfax had?

SOLO:

(*Holding up card or writing on blackboard: 1748-52—Surveyor*):

Seventeen hundred forty-eight . . .
when he was still a lad.

SCENE 3

AT RISE: LORD FAIRFAX *and* LAWRENCE *enter.* LAWRENCE *takes a paper from his pocket, holds it out.*

LAWRENCE: What do you think of this, Lord Fairfax?

LORD FAIRFAX: What is it? (*Peers at paper, takes small magnifying glass from pocket*) A map?

LAWRENCE: Do you recognize it?

LORD FAIRFAX (*Studying paper*): A map of the South Meadow here at Mount Vernon, is it not? Very carefully done. Neat. Accurate, as far as I can judge. Excellent workmanship. Did your young brother George do it? I have seen him with his instruments, again and again.

LAWRENCE: Yes, George did it. Amazing, how serious he is about his maps. For a lad not quite sixteen . . .

LORD FAIRFAX: He has skill. Ambition. Patience. Self-discipline. I have been wondering, Lawrence, about the thousands of acres of wilderness I own west of the Blue Ridge Mountains. Settlers are moving in, taking what land they want, cutting timber, building cabins. I feel I should have my boundaries marked, to establish ownership. Do you think George would care to help?

LAWRENCE: Do I think . . . ! There he comes now, Lord

Fairfax, over the hill. I am sure he can answer your question better than I. (*Calls*) George! Over here, George!

LORD FAIRFAX (*Looking at map again*): A nice piece of work. Very nice indeed. (GEORGE *enters with tripod.*)

GEORGE: Good morning, Lawrence. And Lord Fairfax, sir.

LAWRENCE: Lord Fairfax has a question to ask you, George.

GEORGE: To ask *me?*

LORD FAIRFAX: And not about fox-hunting, either. Or horses. (*Clears throat*) You are interested in surveying, I notice . . .

GEORGE: Yes, sir. Very much, sir.

LORD FAIRFAX: And how far along are you?

GEORGE: I still have a great deal to learn. But I'm not *too* bad, am I, Lawrence?

LORD FAIRFAX: Would you be able to start in three weeks? On March 11, say?

GEORGE: Start what, sir?

LORD FAIRFAX: I am planning to have my wilderness lands surveyed. Would you care to be one of the party? I will pay you well.

GEORGE (*Eagerly*): Would I! Would I, sir! Oh, let me get some of my maps to show you . . . (*He runs out.* LAWRENCE *and* LORD FAIRFAX, *amused, follow.*)

CHORUS: George Washington marches on!

* * *

CHORUS:

When did Mount Vernon come to him—
his brother's large estate?

SOLO:

(*Holding up card or writing on blackboard: 1752—Gets Mt. Vernon*):

Seventeen hundred fifty-two,
dropped from the hands of fate.

SCENE 4

AT RISE: ANNE FAIRFAX WASHINGTON *and* GEORGE *enter, talking earnestly.*

ANNE: I need your help, George.

GEORGE: You know I will do anything I can, Anne. But I cannot bring Lawrence back . . . or your little daughter. To think of losing them both, so close together!

ANNE: Within a few weeks of each other. That was July. Now it is November, and the ache is still in my heart. They say that time heals all sorrows. But, oh, how slowly, George.

GEORGE: I know. I miss Lawrence too, more than I can say. He was so much more to me than a half-brother. Had he been full brother and father combined, I could not have loved him more.

ANNE: I am glad you had those months with him in the Bahamas last winter . . . though I missed him terribly at the time.

GEORGE: We were so hopeful the mild air would help him. And for a while it did, you know. But (*Giving gesture of despair*) . . . And so young, only thirty-four.

ANNE (*After a pause*): George, I want your advice—as a brother-in-law, not as one of the executors of the estate. Lawrence left you a large interest in Mount Vernon, and you have always loved the place. Don't you think you should take it over? I have no wish to be burdened with so many acres of farm land. I know nothing about farming.

GEORGE (*Figuring on back of envelope*): No place in the world means more to me than Mount Vernon. But, as Lawrence's wife, you must have a fair return. (*Figures*) How would it be if I paid you eighty thousand pounds of tobacco yearly?

ANNE: Isn't eighty thousand pounds of tobacco a great deal, George?

GEORGE: I would gladly pay it.

ANNE: You are more than fair. You are generous! And it will be such a load off my mind to know you are here, carrying on as master of Mount Vernon. You will be very busy, George . . . with all those acres, and Lawrence's wish for you to enter the militia . . . and the House of Burgesses.

GEORGE: Yes, I shall be very busy. But that is exactly what I like. And now, shall we go check the accounts? (*They exit*)

CHORUS: Washington marches on!

* * *

CHORUS:

When did he fight in what is called
the French and Indian War?

SOLO:

(*Holding up card or writing on blackboard: 1754-8, French & Indian War*):

Seventeen fifty-four to eight,
with hardships by the score.

SCENE 5

AT RISE: GENERAL BRADDOCK, *brandishing his sword, crosses stage excitedly.*

BRADDOCK (*Shouting*): Hold ranks! Hold ranks! Take the fire of the enemy like men. I command you to hold ranks. (GEORGE WASHINGTON *rushes in to catch up with* GENERAL BRADDOCK.)

WASHINGTON: General Braddock! General Braddock . . . if you will order the men to scatter, sir . . . Let them meet

the enemy under cover instead of out in the open. I know
how these Indians and French fight, from behind trees . . .

BRADDOCK (*Striding out*): My men will stand in ranks, Washington, as they are bidden, without breach of discipline.
(*Exits*)

WASHINGTON: But, sir . . . (*Exits after* BRADDOCK. *Three*
SOLDIERS *stagger in.*)

1ST SOLDIER: Let's get out of here, anywhere. Anywhere!

2ND SOLDIER: Where did the shots come from? Did you see
the enemy?

3RD SOLDIER: The shots come from all directions. No one
sees the enemy.

1ST SOLDIER: We make easy targets in our red coats.

2ND SOLDIER: Did you see Braddock's aide-de-camp, Colonel
Washington? He strode among us soldiers, calm as ice,
trying to get us to retreat in orderly fashion. His horse
was shot out from under him.

1ST SOLDIER: Aye, and he mounted another.

2ND SOLDIER: Men were slaughtered all around him, but he
wasn't even wounded.

3RD SOLDIER: I could follow a man like that! Would to heaven
he were in charge here. (*They stagger out.*)

CHORUS: Washington marches on!

*　　*　　*

CHORUS:

When did he marry, settle down
on the land he loved so well?

SOLO:

(*Holding up card or writing on blackboard: 1759-75, Farmer*):

Seventeen hundred fifty-nine,
a happy date to tell.

Scene 6

AT RISE: MARY BALL WASHINGTON *comes in with sewing, sits and works. Soon* BETTY WASHINGTON LEWIS *hurries in with newspapers. She greets her mother affectionately, and takes off wraps as she talks.*

BETTY: Oh, Mama, have you seen the papers—from Fredericksburg and Alexandria? I was afraid you hadn't, so I took the ferry over . . . I couldn't wait to show you.

MRS. WASHINGTON: About George's wedding?

BETTY: Yes, look! (*Shows a paper*) A long account, and so glowing, Mama. The charming and beautiful young widow, Martha Custis, and the handsome and gallant young officer, George Washington!

MRS. WASHINGTON (*Looking at paper*): She will be a great help to George in many ways. Perhaps I should not say it out loud . . . but I can't help thinking that her fortune will not come amiss. I hear it is a large one.

BETTY (*Sitting down*): And, imagine, a ready-made family for George! Jacky six, and Patsy four. I can imagine how he loves them.

MRS. WASHINGTON (*Reading*): "In the church where the wedding was solemnized there was a bright show of resplendent uniforms with their gold lace and scarlet coats. Later the bridegroom, himself clad in shining blue and silver and scarlet, rode beside the coach that bore his bride homeward . . ." (*Looks up*) George has done well, Betty. I always knew he would.

BETTY: And remember how he wanted to go to sea? And how Uncle Joseph agreed with you that he shouldn't?

MRS. WASHINGTON: Indeed I remember. How different his life would have been! Come, let us move closer to the grate. There is a January chill in the air today. (*They exit.*)

CHORUS: Washington marches on!

*   *   *

CHORUS:

When did the Revolution start—
that placed him in command.

SOLO:

(*Holding up card or writing on blackboard: 1775-83, Commander-in-chief*):

Seventeen seventy-five.   In June
he took the task in hand.

SCENE 7

AT RISE: JOHN ADAMS *enters, takes place behind table.*

VOICE FROM AUDIENCE: Sh! John Adams is about to speak. Sh!

ADAMS: Gentlemen of the second Continental Congress,— We are agreed that we must prepare to defend ourselves against British tyranny immediately.   To my mind the choice of commander of the continental armies is easy enough.   There is no soldier in America to be compared with Colonel George Washington of Virginia, either in experience or distinction.   He is gallant, straightforward, earnest.   (*Looks up*) Did I glimpse the Colonel leaving the room in confusion just now?   Run after him, attendant. Bring him back!   (*Resumes speech.*)   I move that Congress, meeting here in solemn assembly in Philadelphia, put the gentleman from Virginia in charge of the American army! (*Cheers, shouts of "Aye, aye" from audience.*)   His skill and experience as an officer, his independent fortune, great talents, and excellent universal character, would unite the colonies better than any other person in the union." (*More cheers from audience, calls for "George Washington!" and "Colonel Washington."* WASHINGTON *enters slowly.* JOHN ADAMS *steps up, escorts him to table, then sits down.*)

WASHINGTON: I beg it to be remembered by every gentleman in this room, that I this day declare with the utmost sincerity I do not think myself equal to the command I am honored with. I cannot refuse a call to serve my country. As to pay, I will have none of it. I do not wish to make any profit from the war. I shall keep an accounting of my expenses, and that is all I desire. (*Cheers from audience.* JOHN ADAMS *grasps* WASHINGTON'S *hand, and they exit together.*)

CHORUS: Washington marches on!

* * *

CHORUS:

Month after month the army fought,
and often on the run!
Month after month of toil and trial,
and never a battle won.

SOLO:

(*Holding up card or writing on blackboard: 1776, Crosses Delaware*):

Then on a bitter Christmas night
Washington staged a famous fight.

SCENE 8

AT RISE: *Two* SENTRIES *enter, pace back and forth.*

1ST SENTRY: No morning ever has gone more slowly. (*Slaps arms to keep warm.*) How soon do you think they will send back news?

2ND SENTRY: For the hundredth time, don't expect news till noonday, at the earliest. (*Looks at watch*) Eleven o'clock. Calm down, brother.

1ST SENTRY: If only I could have gone along.

2ND SENTRY: Someone had to stay behind to guard the camp. You and I are as good as the next. (*Stomps feet*) It's blasted cold.

1ST SENTRY: Noonday at the earliest?

2ND SENTRY: Look here. They didn't leave till after midnight. (*He shudders*) And *what* a Christmas midnight! Sleet. Bitter cold. The Delaware choked with cakes of floating ice. Do you think it a quick and easy task to transport 2400 men across the river on such a night? Even with the best planning?

1ST SENTRY: They say General Washington had it all worked out to the smallest detail.

2ND SENTRY: Naturally. Still, after the crossing, they had to march nine miles through snow and cold to Trenton. You think that can be done in a moment?

1ST SENTRY: No . . . ooo.

2ND SENTRY: I say if they arrived at Trenton an hour after sunrise they did well. And *then*. You expect they could march right in and take the town? Against those well-armed German soldiers the British hired to guard it? (*Pounds hands together*) You expect too much.

1ST SENTRY: I am counting on Christmas. I am counting on those Hessians drinking too much, and celebrating too much, last night.

2ND SENTRY: Even so, taking a town is not easy. And have you reason to suppose our luck has changed? Retreat. Retreat. Retreat. That has been our record. Have we won a battle yet—answer me that?

1ST SENTRY (*Grudgingly*): No . . . ooo. But this! We are

all fired with the wish to give General Washington a Christmas present. A victory—at last.

2ND SENTRY: A wish. That's all very well. But wishes don't win battles. Though heaven knows a victory is a Christmas present that would warm all our hearts. (*Bitterly*) They need warming. (*Stomps*) And not only our hearts.

1ST SENTRY: Noonday!

2ND SENTRY: Remember, a messenger would have to get back the nine miles from Trenton, and cross the river again. After the battle.

1ST SENTRY (*Stubbornly*): If the victory were a quick one . . . (*They pace back and forth in silence. In a few moments a* MESSENGER *runs in.*)

SENTRIES (*Challenging him*): Halt! Who goes there?

MESSENGER (*Saluting*): Messenger from General Washington in Trenton.

SENTRIES (*Eagerly*): Speak up, lad. What news?

MESSENGER: We crossed the river on the barges without mishap, in spite of the sleet and bumping ice.

1ST SENTRY: Yes, yes, you crossed the river. But the battle? Do we hold Trenton?

MESSENGER: We marched the nine miles without mishap, arriving after sun-up, deploying to enter by different roads.

2ND SENTRY: Naturally, by different roads. We know the General had it all planned. But the Hessians? Did they put up a good fight?

MESSENGER: There was no place for them to run. They were dazed, drugged from too much celebrating last night. We had no losses to speak of.

SENTRIES: And the Hessians?

MESSENGER: They lost their commander and forty-one others —dead. It was all over in less than an hour. We captured thirty officers and more than a thousand men.

SENTRIES (*Throwing up their hats*): A victory! A victory!

A Christmas present for General Washington! Come, let's tell the others. (*Go out with* MESSENGER) Our first victory in the war . . .

CHORUS: Washington marches on!

* * *

CHORUS:

Success was brief. Then more retreat
through countryside and gorge.
What was the time that tried men's souls?

SOLO:

(*Holding up card or writing on blackboard: 1777-8, Valley Forge*):

The winter at Valley Forge.

SCENE 9

AT RISE: MARTHA WASHINGTON *enters with knitting, sits and works busily.* GENERAL WASHINGTON *enters, paces back and forth deep in thought.*

MARTHA: You are worried, George. (*Pause*) Are you angry with me for coming? After you wrote that I would be much more comfortable at Mount Vernon?

WASHINGTON (*Going to her affectionately*): No. No. I am not angry with you, Martha. Assuredly you *would* be more comfortable at Mount Vernon. Valley Forge is not renowned for its comforts! But you have been a cheering note in a bleak landscape ever since you came, my dear. The soldiers feel it. Especially the sick and wounded you so kindly visit.

MARTHA: Oh, I'm glad.

WASHINGTON: And the ones who get the socks you knit think you are an angel from heaven! I wonder if you realize how much a pair of warm socks means in Valley Forge?

MARTHA: I think so, George.

GEORGE (*Bursting out impatiently*): Socks . . . mittens . . . coats . . . shoes . . . uniforms . . . *why* don't we get our supplies? Bread . . . meat . . . ammunition . . . guns . . . we need everything, Martha. Everything! That's why I am worried. Congress is so disorganized and inefficient. Why, these days, we scarcely have what can be called a government.

MARTHA: I suppose the British moving into Philadelphia didn't help matters. You say Congress is in exile at York. It has probably lost heart. (*Hastily*) Though, of course, I understand nothing about politics.

WASHINGTON: Lost heart! Lost head, I should say. (*Paces angrily*) And to think that just twenty miles from here General Howe and his officers are having a gay winter social season in Philadelphia! His men are warm and well-fed. They live in ease and comfort. While my men are starving and freezing! Yet naked as they are, Martha (*There is a catch in his voice*) . . . they show incomparable patience and loyalty. Ah, Thomas Paine is right . . . this is indeed a time that tries men's souls. Mine included.

MARTHA: Is there no way out?

WASHINGTON: None that I can see at the moment, unless Congress can pull itself together. How can we have an army without supplies? And the men have not been paid for months! (ORDERLY *enters, salutes.*)

ORDERLY: The Marquis de Lafayette to see you, sir.

WASHINGTON: Lafayette! Show him in immediately.

MARTHA (*Rising*): Perhaps I should leave . . .

WASHINGTON: Not until you have greeted our young friend, Martha. He, too, is a bright light on a bleak horizon. (LAFAYETTE *enters, salutes. He and* GENERAL WASHINGTON *greet each other affectionately.*) My dear Lafayette!

LAFAYETTE: General Washington!

WASHINGTON: You have met my wife once before. (*She and*

LAFAYETTE *bow*) The soldiers here call her Lady Washington.

MARTHA (*Smiling at* LAFAYETTE *as she exits*) : It is my reward for darning their socks, Marquis!

LAFAYETTE : I could not wait to bring you the news, sir.

WASHINGTON : News?

LAFAYETTE (*Taking letter from inner pocket*) : A secret letter, from friends in France. There is every reason to believe that France will soon declare war on England, and support our cause with money and supplies.

WASHINGTON : Can it be true! Soon, you say?

LAFAYETTE (*Showing letter*) : Very soon. Indeed, I am informed that a handsome sum of money is already on the way.

WASHINGTON (*Much relieved*) : What is it they say . . . that it is always darkest just before the dawn? Come, we must tell Martha. (*They exit.*)

CHORUS : Washington marches on!

* * *

CHORUS :

Year after year the war dragged on,
the verdict still not won.
And then the battle of Yorktown came.

SOLO :

(*Holding up card or writing on blackboard: 1781, Yorktown*) :

Seventeen eighty-one.

SCENE 10

AT RISE : NEWSBOYS *run across stage shouting, waving papers.*

1ST NEWSBOY : Extra! Extra! Cornwallis surrenders after three-week siege. Washington takes 8000 men. Victory! Victory! (*Exits*)

2ND NEWSBOY: The most decisive battle of the war. Washington wins at Yorktown. The war is over! (*Exits*)

CHORUS: Washington marches on!

* * *

CHORUS:

But still a treaty to be signed
before our land was free!

SOLO:

The General had to keep command
till seventeen eighty-three.

CHORUS:

And then, at Christmas, home again!
Mount Vernon. Home, at last.

SOLO:

(*Holding up card or writing on blackboard: 1784-8, Farmer*)

Seventeen eighty-four to eight.
And, oh, the time went fast.

SCENE 11

AT RISE: WASHINGTON *enters, sits at table, begins to write.*

WASHINGTON (*Writing*): To the Marquis de Lafayette, many greetings. At length, my dear Marquis, I am become a private citizen on the banks of the Potomac; and under the shadow of my own vine and my own fig-tree, free from the bustle of a camp and the busy scenes of public life, I am solacing myself with those tranquil enjoyments of which a soldier can have very little conception. I have not only retired from all public employments, but I am retiring within myself . . . (NELLY CUSTIS *comes in a little tentatively.*)

NELLY: Grandfather. Grandfather, you promised to show me the new little colt . . . (WASHINGTON *smiles, puts down quill, and goes out with* NELLY.)

CHORUS: Washington marches on!

* * *

CHORUS:

When was he called to serve again?
Washington, President!

SOLO:

(*Holding up card or writing on blackboard: 1789-97, President*):

Seventeen hundred eighty-nine.
Two terms, eight years, he spent.

SCENE 12

AT RISE: CHANCELLOR LIVINGSTON, *carrying a Bible, and* GEORGE WASHINGTON *enter.*

LIVINGSTON (*Holding out Bible*): Do you solemnly swear that you will faithfully execute the office of President of the United States, and will, to the best of your ability, preserve, protect, and defend the Constitution of the United States?

WASHINGTON: I do solemnly swear that I will faithfully execute the office of President of the United States, and will, to the best of my ability, preserve, protect and defend the Constitution of the United States. (*Bends to kiss Bible. Then, solemnly, with bowed head* . . .) So help me, God.

LIVINGSTON (*To audience*): Long live George Washington, President of the United States!

AUDIENCE (*Cheering*): Long live George Washington. Long

live the father of our country. Hail to the first President of the United States. (WASHINGTON *and* LIVINGSTON *exit.*)

1ST VOICE FROM AUDIENCE: Did you hear? He won't accept a salary as President.

2ND VOICE: Nor did he take a salary all those years he was commander-in-chief.

3RD VOICE: Imagine, he fears he is not good enough for the post!

4TH VOICE: Who *would* be good enough if he isn't?

SEVERAL: No one. No one in our thirteen States.

5TH VOICE: Poor man, we snatch him away from Mount Vernon again. We demand much of him.

SEVERAL: We need him. We need him!

AUDIENCE: Long live George Washington, President of the United States!

CHORUS: Washington marches on!

*   *   *

CHORUS:

When did he die, George Washington?

SOLO:

(*Holding up card or writing on blackboard: 1799—Died*):

Seventeen ninety-nine.

CHORUS:

But he still lives on in our minds and hearts, and will till the end of time!

SCENE 13

AT RISE: SCHOOLMASTER *enters, with books.*

SCHOOLMASTER: Boys of the Latin School of Fredericksburg, sad news has just reached us from Mount Vernon, this

December day. George Washington is dead! The father of our country is dead.

He was our friend . . . almost our neighbor, when he lived across the river at Ferry Farm years ago. And many of you remember his mother when she lived on Charles Street next door to her daughter and grandchildren.

George Washington is dead. In him were united such qualities of greatness as seldom appear in one man. How long he served our country! How well he served it—as soldier, patriot, statesman, citizen!

Boys, open your copy books and write these words on the title page where you will see them often: "George Washington—first in war, first in peace, and first in the hearts of his countrymen."

Our beloved commander-in-chief, our first President, is dead. But he will never be forgotten. Other heroes, other statesmen, will come and go, but the memory of George Washington is here to stay. (*Nods solemnly, and exits*)

CHORUS: Washington marches on!

* * *

SCENE 14

BEFORE CURTAIN: *A procession of boys and girls of the present generation march across the stage carrying flags, chanting:* "Washington marches on!"

THE END

When Freedom Was News

Characters

NEWSSTAND OPERATOR
1ST GIRL (*Publick Occurrences, Boston, 1690*)*
1ST BOY (*News-Letter, Boston, 1704*)
POLICEMAN
NEWSBOY
2ND GIRL (*New England Courant, Boston, 1721*)
2ND BOY (*New York Weekly Journal, 1733*)
3RD BOY (*Evening Post, Boston, 1735*)
3RD GIRL (*Gazette, Boston, 1755*)
4TH BOY (*McDougall's Handbill, 1770*)

* BOYS *and* GIRLS *representing newspapers wear "sandwich boards" with name of paper and date in large print, and newspaper copy below.*

TIME: *The present. Late at night.*

SETTING: *A street corner in New York City.*

AT RISE: NEWSSTAND OPERATOR *is closing up for the night, whistling as he works. He weighs down unsold papers with a brick, puts coin container in handy place, conceals some magazines under the stand. When he is finished, he pulls down cap and walks offstage.* 1ST BOY *and* 1ST GIRL *have been lurking in the shadows. Cautiously they tiptoe toward stand.*

1st GIRL (*Pointing at one paper after another*): Look at these papers, will you! The size of them! Do you know how big I was when I appeared in public two hundred and fifty years ago?

1st BOY: Probably about the same size I was. Smaller than a sheet of typewriting paper.

1st GIRL: And the thickness of them! (*Thumbs through a New York Times*) Forty-five pages in this *New York Times*. All I had was four pages, and not even enough printing to fill them.

1st BOY: Look at the ads, will you! I had only one ad in my first issue. And some of these pages are half pictures! Do you know that I carried the very first picture printed in an American newspaper? In 1707.

1st GIRL: I suppose it was a picture of Queen Anne.

1st BOY: No. It was the picture of a flag—a little British flag.

1st GIRL (*Still looking at papers*): I've looked at the first page of all these papers, and I can't find a single mention of a license.

1st BOY: You can't? (*Looks too*) That's funny. Do you suppose they are all defying the government? Why, without a license, these papers are likely to be suppressed any minute!

1st GIRL: The way *I* was. (*Footsteps are heard offstage. Boy and GIRL listen.*) Someone's coming. It looks like a policeman!

1st BOY: Maybe he's coming to padlock this newsstand for the government because the papers were printed without a license. Let's hide! (*They run to shadows again. POLICEMAN enters, ambles over to newsstand, scans headlines, swings stick, and walks out unconcerned. BOY and GIRL tiptoe back.*)

1st GIRL: He didn't do a thing.

1st BOY: Maybe he can't read.

1st GIRL: Maybe he needs glasses. My goodness, if he read this headline, he would have been up in arms! Listen to the way this paper complains against the government. (*Reads*) "Officials to blame for crime wave. Public demands protection."

1st BOY: How do they get away with it? (NEWSBOY *shouting offstage, "Extry. Extry."*)

1st GIRL: Shall we hide?

1st BOY: From a newsboy? Never. He's a distant relative of ours. Maybe we can find out something. (NEWSBOY *comes in with papers.*)

NEWSBOY: Extry! Governor involved in tax scandal. Read all about it.

1st BOY: Say . . . you'll be put in jail for selling a paper like that!

NEWSBOY: Me? How come? This is a free country, isn't it?

1st GIRL: You can't sell a paper that complains against the Governor.

NEWSBOY: Since when can't I? You should see the papers I sell. (*Taps papers*) This is nothing! (*Looks at* BOY *and* GIRL *curiously*) Say, where have you been all your life? (*Reads date on* BOY's *paper*) 1704! (*Reads date on* GIRL's *paper*) 1690! Well, you certainly are back numbers, aren't you? 'Way out of date. What do you know? You're from way back when America was a handful of colonies under the thumb of the British.

1st BOY: I'm the Boston *News-Letter,* the first American newspaper.

1st GIRL: Wait a minute. *I'm* the first American newspaper. I came before you did. 1690—that's my date. You can see for yourself.

NEWSBOY (*Reading masthead*): "Publick Occurrences, Both Foreign and Domestick. Boston, September 25, 1690." (*Laughs*) That's some name for a newspaper. I'll say you're an antique—in capital letters. (*Turns to* BOY) What about you? (*Reads*) "*News-Letter,* Boston, April 17, 1704." I'm not much good at arithmetic, but 1704 is certainly later than 1690 any way you figure it. What do you mean, you're the first newspaper?

1ST BOY: That's easy. I lived and she didn't. I lived for quite a few years. She was only one day old when the government clamped down on her. She doesn't really count.

NEWSBOY (*Looking at some of* GIRL'S *news items*): Pretty dull reading, these "publick occurrences, both foreign and domestick." No wonder you didn't make a go of it, sister. People like their news jazzed up a little . . .

1ST GIRL: Oh, it wasn't because of my news. *That* wasn't why I lived only a day. It was because of my publisher's announcement . . . here . . . (*Points to place on sandwich board*) . . . read it.

NEWSBOY (*Reads to himself, looks up puzzled*): I don't see anything wrong with what that says. All newspapers are supposed to expose things that are wrong. All newspapers want to direct the thoughts of their readers, and help them understand "the circumstances of Publick Affairs."

1ST BOY: That's what *you* think. But what about getting a license?

NEWSBOY: What license?

1ST GIRL: Why, a license to print a newspaper.

NEWSBOY: Never heard of it. (BOY *and* GIRL *look at each other in amazement.*)

1ST GIRL: You never heard of a license? That was my

downfall. Because my publisher said he was going to expose things that were wrong, the government wouldn't give him a license. So . . . (*Throws up hands*) that was the last of me.

NEWSBOY: I'd like to see the government get away with that nowadays in the good old U.S.A. Why, it's unheard of! People wouldn't stand for it. They wouldn't stand for the government running the newspapers, telling them what they can print and what they can't. (*To* 1ST BOY) Did you have to get a license from the government too?

1ST BOY: I certainly did. And I had to be mighty careful about what I said, believe me. Even after newspapers no longer had to get a license—around 1720, I think— they weren't free to say what they thought.

NEWSBOY: This is all news to me! I'm going to tell the City Editor to put you in a special edition, that's what I'm going to do. (*Merrily*) Extry! Extry! Old newspapers led a dog's life. Couldn't run without a license! (*Goes out laughing*)

1ST GIRL: Times certainly have changed.

1ST BOY: I guess we're back numbers, all right. (2ND GIRL *comes running in, frightened.*)

2ND GIRL: Did you see him? Did you see him?

1ST GIRL AND BOY: Who? The newsboy?

2ND GIRL: The policeman! I like to give policemen a wide berth. Ever since my publisher was put in jail . . .

1ST GIRL (*Looking at masthead*): "New England Courant, August 7, 1721." Hello! You're one of us, aren't you. A has-been. An antique.

1ST BOY: Say, you don't have to worry about the policeman. He doesn't even *know* about licenses.

2ND GIRL: Oh, I'm not worrying about that. Licenses were done away with before I saw the light of day.

1ST GIRL: But didn't you say your publisher was put in jail?

2ND GIRL: I did. And do you know why? Because he printed an anonymous letter hinting that the government wasn't protecting the coast against pirates. It was true, too.

1ST BOY: Who was your publisher?

2ND GIRL: James Franklin, in Boston.

1ST BOY: He was Benjamin Franklin's brother, wasn't he?

2ND GIRL (*Nodding*): He taught Benjamin Franklin the printing business. And Benjamin taught his brother a few things, too, I'd say. When James Franklin was put in jail for printing that little remark about the government, Benjamin got out the *Courant* all by himself. He was only sixteen years old, but was full of lively ideas. Like making up the Dogood letters. Look, I've got one of them here. (*Points to board*)

1ST GIRL (*Looking*): The letter is signed Silence Dogood.

2ND GIRL: That's just a name Benjamin Franklin made up. He wrote every word of the letters. (POLICEMAN *appears at side of stage, watching curiously.*)

1ST BOY (*Peering at letter, reading*): "There can be no such thing . . . as public liberty without freedom of speech; which is the right of every man as far as by it he does not hurt or control the right of another; and this is the only check it ought to suffer . . ."

POLICEMAN (*Advancing*): What's going on here?

2ND GIRL (*Frightened*): Oh! (*Draws back*) But they said you were different.

POLICEMAN: Different? What's that you're reading?

1ST BOY (*Pointing to Dogood letter*): Benjamin Franklin
wrote it, sir. There's more. What do you think of it?

POLICEMAN (*Reading slowly*): "Whoever would overthrow the liberty of a nation must begin by subduing
the freeness of speech . . ." Why, everyone knows that.
Look what happened in Germany under Hitler.

BOY AND GIRLS: Germany? Hitler?

1ST GIRL: You see, sir, we're slightly out of date.

POLICEMAN: Well, you must be—not to have heard of
Hitler. In order to stay in power in Germany he had to
muzzle the newspapers and tell people what to think.
Where have you been all your life? (*Sees mastheads and
dates*) 1690! 1704! 1721! Why, that was before there
even was a United States! When the colonies were governed by England. Look here, did you escape from a
museum or something?

1ST BOY: We just came out to catch up with the times,
sir. We won't hurt anything. Honest, we won't. We'll
be back where we belong in the morning.

POLICEMAN: So people were worrying about freedom of
the press when Benjamin Franklin was a lad . . . way
back then!

2ND GIRL: Do *you* put many publishers in jail?

POLICEMAN: Publishers? I never knew one to crack a safe
or kill a man. I can't remember jailing a single publisher.

BOY AND GIRLS: Not even when they criticize the government?

POLICEMAN: Why shouldn't they criticize the government,
if there's cause for complaint? There's no law against
criticizing the government in these United States.

2ND GIRL: Well, there used to be. And I ought to know.

POLICEMAN: What's freedom of speech for if you can't say or write what you think? (2ND BOY *and* 3RD BOY *come in at one side, see newsstand, go to look at it. They look around for a street sign, approach others.*)

2ND BOY: Pardon me, can you tell us if this is the corner of Nassau and Wall Streets?

POLICEMAN: Absolutely correct. Looking for someone?

3RD BOY: Not someone, but something. Where's the courthouse?

POLICEMAN: What courthouse?

3RD BOY: Where the famous trial took place. Corner of Nassau and Wall Streets—that's the address. But I don't see anything that looks like my description of the courthouse.

POLICEMAN: What famous trial are you talking about? Say, what goes on around here tonight?

1ST BOY (*Reading mastheads on* 2ND BOY *and* 3RD BOY): "*New York Weekly Journal.* 1733. *Evening Post,* Boston, 1735."

POLICEMAN: You mean there was a famous trial way back then? More than two hundred years ago. And you're looking for the courthouse where the case was tried? What case was it, son?

3RD BOY: The Zenger case.

POLICEMAN: Zenger? Zenger? (*Looks at others*) Any of you ever hear of Zenger? (*They shake their heads.*)

1ST GIRL: But you see, we couldn't. We were before his time.

2ND BOY: John Peter Zenger published the first issue of the *New York Weekly Journal* in November, 1733. (*Taps sandwich board*) That's me. The *Weekly Journal.*

3RD BOY: And let me tell you, every newspaper after that

date owed a lot to Zenger. They wouldn't have got to first base trying to expose bad government if it hadn't been for his fight for freedom of the press.

2ND BOY (*Proudly*): He blazed the trail, Mr. Zenger did.

POLICEMAN (*Scratching his head*): The name sounds familiar, sort of. But I can't for the life of me place the man. You say he published a paper, son?

2ND BOY: What would you think if New York City had only one newspaper, the way it did until 1733? And what would you think if that one paper had to kowtow to the royal governor?

POLICEMAN: I wouldn't like it. I wouldn't like it a bit.

2ND BOY: Well, Mr. Zenger didn't either. He had the nerve to start a second paper, so he could let the people know what a scoundrel the British governor really was. He dared to show up the governor time after time . . . how he was trying to run elections, and handpick judges, and interfere with trial by jury.

1ST GIRL: It's a wonder Mr. Zenger didn't have his ears cut off. That's what they did in England in *my* day, for criticizing the government.

2ND GIRL: Benjamin Franklin's brother was thrown into jail for much less than that. Much less.

POLICEMAN: What happened to this Zenger who dared to speak out?

2ND BOY: They threw him into prison and kept him there for nine months without a trial! And you should have seen the place—a cold, damp little cell that just about ruined Zenger's health. And they wouldn't let him see anybody or have visitors. The only way his wife could talk to him was through a small hole in the door.

POLICEMAN: Couldn't he get out on bail?

2ND BOY: The judges were under the thumb of the governor. They set bail at ten times as much as Zenger owned in the world . . . in order to keep him in jail.

1ST GIRL: I suppose his paper just naturally went out of business, the way I did.

2ND GIRL (*Quickly*): *I* didn't go out of business when James Franklin went to jail. Ben Franklin took over, and he did a good job, too.

2ND BOY: Zenger's paper didn't die, either. He had a smart wife, and she dug right in and ran the paper while her husband was in prison.

3RD BOY: Finally, the big day of the Zenger trial came. Here . . . (*Takes clippings from pocket, passes them around*) . . . here are some reprints. I was the first paper to publish a full account of the Zenger trial. My publisher, Thomas Fleet, defied the authorities in doing it. He was a courageous man, I tell you.

POLICEMAN: What's so remarkable about publishing an account of a trial? We do it every day and think nothing of it. Just the way we print the weather.

3RD BOY: Well, it was something to do in *my* day—a trial like the Zenger trial. My publisher started a precedent, and after that other papers had the courage to follow suit.

1ST BOY (*Inspired from looking at reprint*): Say, this is exciting, this is. Let's have a mock trial. I'll be Zenger's attorney!

3RD BOY: Do you think you can hold forth like a famous lawyer?

1ST BOY (*Striking a pose, reading*): "Free men have the right to complain when they are hurt . . ."

3RD BOY: All right. You'll do. You be Andrew Hamilton,

then. Remember, you're an important lawyer . . . eighty years old . . . the leading lawyer in the colonies. You came all the way from Philadelphia by stagecoach to defend Zenger's right to print the truth. And you did it without charging a cent! (*To* 1ST GIRL) How would you like to be the judge—not that there ever *was* a woman judge back in your time!

1ST GIRL: I'd like to strike a modern note for a change. I'll be the judge.

3RD BOY: Let's see, we need a prosecuting attorney. (*Looks at* POLICEMAN) What about you, sir?

POLICEMAN: Right up my alley. (*Scans reprint*)

3RD BOY: Who'll be foreman of the jury?

2ND BOY: Let me. No one has the Zenger case more at heart than I have—Zenger's own paper.

3RD BOY: All right, then. We are in the courtroom here at Nassau and Wall Streets in New York City. It is a hot August day, in 1735. The judge is on the bench, the jury in the box. The courtroom is crowded to overflowing. Andrew Hamilton is speaking . . .

1ST BOY (*Reading with gusto*): I maintain that John Peter Zenger is not guilty! Free men have a right to protest the abuses of power in the strongest terms . . . to put their neighbors upon their guard . . . Free men have the right to assert with courage the sense they have of the blessings of liberty . . . and their resolve at all hazards to preserve it.

POLICEMAN (*Reading loudly*): That is not the point, Mr. Hamilton. You have confessed that Mr. Zenger published the damaging statements. What more do we need?

1ST BOY: The statements are *true,* Mr. Prosecuting Attorney, and therefore there is no ground for punishment. We will produce witnesses to prove the truth of the statements.

1ST GIRL: As judge of this court, I refuse to hear those witnesses. Truth is no defense to this crime, and never has been.

1ST BOY: Then, your Honor, I shall appeal directly to the jury on behalf of Mr. Zenger. Gentlemen of the Jury, you are citizens of New York, honest and lawful men. The facts which we offer in this case are notoriously known to be true. Therefore in your justice lies our safety. Gentlemen of the Jury, every man who prefers freedom to a life of slavery, will bless and honour you . . . if you uphold Mr. Zenger in this issue of freedom of the press.

1ST GIRL: As Judge of this Court I give the following instructions to the jury. The publication and printing of criticism of the governor have been admitted. Whether the facts are true or not has nothing to do with the case. You will now retire and bring in a verdict—of guilty!

3RD BOY: Will the foreman of the jury please run around the newsstand and return with the verdict? (2ND BOY *runs around stand, comes back, calls out loudly*)

2ND BOY: The jury finds John Peter Zenger NOT GUILTY! (*Everyone cheers, even the prosecuting-attorney* POLICE-MAN)

3RD BOY: So Zenger was free again, free to print the truth and oppose the abuse of power. His trial really made a stir in the colonies, I can tell you. It paved the way for freedom of the press. That's why Zenger is a big name in newspaper history.

POLICEMAN: All very interesting. All very interesting. But I'm afraid this isn't walking my beat—standing around all night on the corner of Wall and Nassau. If I'm not careful somebody will be clapping *me* in jail for something. Well . . . (*Starts to go*) I'll see you in the funny paper. (POLICEMAN *exits.* 3RD GIRL *enters from other side.*)

3RD GIRL: I'm too late! (*Others watch her curiously*) It's all over. Even the shouting.

1ST GIRL: What's all over?

3RD GIRL: The Zenger trial.

3RD BOY: Yes, it's all over. (*Reads masthead on* 3RD GIRL'S *board.*) "Boston *Gazette, 1755.*" You're only twenty years too late, sister. But, let me tell you, the effects of the Zenger case aren't over, even though the trial is. The effects won't *ever* be over, I hope.

3RD GIRL: Thanks to Zenger, the authorities didn't dare muzzle me. I was the first champion of the patriot cause . . . when trouble began with England.

OTHERS: You were?

3RD GIRL: You should see some of the things I carried in my pages! (*Points to board*) Here's a letter from Samuel Adams abusing the British government of the colonies. I published letters from other fiery patriots too . . . John Adams, James Otis, and the rest. If it hadn't been for Zenger, I would have been very short-lived. (4TH BOY *appears at side, listening. Above the printing on his board is the number "45" in large numerals.*) As it was, you can't imagine how outspoken some of those patriots were against the British authorities before the Revolution.

4TH BOY (*Approaching*): You were the first, all right, but in time most of the papers in the colonies sided with the patriots. They printed handbills too. That's what I am —one of Alexander McDougall's handbills of the year

1770. (*Looks around*) Maybe I don't belong here. You're all newspapers. But, well . . . I landed Alexander McDougall in jail, I did.

OTHERS: Then you belong here, all right!

1ST GIRL: What did McDougall say that was so awful?

4TH BOY: Some pretty fiery words against quartering British troops on the colonists in New York.

1ST BOY: What's that big "45" at the top of your printing? And it's on each side of your three-cornered hat, too!

2ND GIRL: What does it mean—45?

4TH BOY: That was a great number with the patriots of New York, I can tell you. You see, the Assembly decided McDougall's handbill was rebellious. They made a record of their decision on page 45 of the journal of their proceedings. After that the local patriots used 45 as their password. (*Takes out calling cards, passes them around.*) Here, have one of McDougall's calling cards.

3RD BOY (*Looking at card*): Is this a joke? It looks like a calling card to come to *jail*.

4TH BOY: That's right. That's just what it is. McDougall had the cards printed in the local papers because so many visitors flocked to see him in jail.

2ND GIRL (*Reading*): "At home to my friends at the New Gaol from three o'clock in the afternoon until six." (*Laughs*)

2ND BOY: Zenger should see this. After the way they treated him . . . locking him up in a cell and not letting him have any visitors.

4TH BOY: McDougall was the first American patriot to be imprisoned by the British. On the 45th day of the year 1770, his patriot friends staged a feast at the jail. They served 45 beefsteaks cut from bullocks 45 months old!

And that was only part of it. There was 45 of this, and 45 of that.

2ND BOY: And poor Zenger almost starved to death in jail.

4TH BOY: Times changed pretty fast after Zenger was declared not guilty. Free speech and a free press came to mean something that the British government of the colonies didn't dare suppress. (NEWSBOY *heard offstage calling, "Extry. Extry."*)

2ND BOY: Who's that?

1ST BOY: Just a friend of ours. Nothing to worry about. (*Calls out eagerly*) Is it about us? A special edition about us . . . the way you said?

NEWSBOY (*Coming in with papers*): Read all about it . . .

1ST GIRL: About the licenses and things?

NEWSBOY: Naw. I talked it over with the City Editor. And you know what he said? Said the issue was dead as a dodo. Said we'd been having freedom of speech so long nobody could even remember when we didn't have it. That goes for freedom of press and religion and assembly, too. It's part of the Constitution, even, part of the Bill of Rights.

2ND BOY: What's the Constitution?

2ND GIRL: What's the Bill of Rights?

NEWSBOY: It's our government set-up. It tells how the United States is governed. But, of course, you wouldn't know about the United States, would you, 'way back then? (BOYS *and* GIRLS *shake their heads*)

NEWSBOY: Well, let me tell you one thing about the Bill of Rights, and you can put it down as the biggest extra-special edition in the world. It gives us four great freedoms: Freedom of worship. Freedom of speech. Freedom of the press. And freedom of holding meetings. And our government can't take any of them away.

BOYS AND GIRLS: Times certainly do change.

NEWSBOY: We've got the freedoms. But, quoting my City Editor, we can lose them if we take them for granted. We've got to be willing to fight for our freedoms . . . we've got to be willing to go to jail if necessary.

2ND GIRL: Like James Franklin.

2ND BOY: And Zenger.

4TH BOY: And McDougall.

3RD BOY: And the rest of the patriots who suffered to gain freedom for their day and ours.

3RD GIRL: Three cheers for freedom won, and kept, and cherished! (*All cheer*)

3RD BOY (*To* NEWSBOY): No one is ever going to take away your freedom if you just remember what people chanted in the taverns and on the streets during the Zenger trial:

BOYS AND GIRLS:

> We are the lads who dare resist
> All autocratic power.
> If you'd help, come on enlist,
> This is the fateful hour.
> In freedom's cause we'll take our stand
> And that's because we love this land
> With a Fa la la la.

(*They march off chanting.*)

THE END

A Dish of Green Peas

Characters

MATTIE
MISS FRAUNCES
ORDERLY
VAN STARN
THOMAS HICKEY

SCENE 1

TIME: *Mid-June, 1776.*

SETTING: *The kitchen of a large house on an estate near New York City, where General Washington has his headquarters.*

AT RISE: MATTIE *and* MISS FRAUNCES *are working in the kitchen, keeping busy at various tasks.*

MATTIE: 'Tis men have the only real chance to help their country, Miss Fraunces. Me, now. I'm dead set against the British—the way they think they can pull us around by the nose, like a prize pig, you might say. But what can a girl do? Or a woman, either?

MISS FRAUNCES: You don't have to carry a gun, Mattie. It never was a woman's part to be flashy about her doings, and it probably never will be.

MATTIE: Trouble is, she never has a chance to *do* any doin's.

MISS FRAUNCES: I'd say you can do more than most right now, Mattie. There isn't another girl in America with your chance to make things comfortable for General Washington. As long as he's here at Mortier House we can feel we're doing our part in a womanly way.

MATTIE (*Sniffing*): Scrubbin' and cleanin' and cookin' and washin' dishes! Oh, I'm not complaining of the work, mind you. Only it's so piddling small, Miss Fraunces. 'Tis a sorry lot the women have compared to the men up in the thick of things.

MISS FRAUNCES: I'm proud to think General Washington wanted me for his housekeeper. I don't count it so piddling to make it pleasant for him here.

MATTIE: He'd 'a missed a chance *not* having you for his housekeeper, after all the trainin' you got at your father's tavern. Everybody knows of the Fraunces Tavern in New York City—that's how famous it is. But, Miss Fraunces, if I was a man now . . . I could be learnin' how to take aim at a Redcoat.

MISS FRAUNCES: There may be more than one way to do that.

MATTIE: What way?

MISS FRAUNCES: You never know.

MATTIE: Not cleanin' and cookin'!

MISS FRAUNCES: I'm not so sure, Mattie. You know how strong the Tories are. Why, I've heard that a third of the colonists are loyal to England and King George. A third, mind you. And New York is the very worst. It occurs to me that we women may have a better chance than men to smell out the enemy.

MATTIE: How? Peelin' potatoes and shuckin' peas?

MISS FRAUNCES: We must keep our eyes open and our ears open and our hearts strong. And our courage up. No one can do more than that. (*There is a knock at inner door.*) Come in!

ORDERLY (*At door*): Oh, Miss Fraunces. General Washington asked me to tell you how much he enjoyed the green peas at dinner last night.

MISS FRAUNCES: I'm so glad. They are just in season now.

ORDERLY: Speaking on my own, I believe the General would enjoy them again . . . and again . . . if they aren't too much trouble. They are one of his favorite dishes.

MATTIE: No trouble a-tall, Orderly . . . a-shuckin' a bushel of peas!

MISS FRAUNCES: Of course, he shall have them again. As a matter of fact, I've already told Mr. Van Starn to bring us more as soon as he picks them.

ORDERLY: The General is grateful for all the things you do to make him comfortable.

MISS FRAUNCES: Thank you. I only wish we could do more.

MATTIE: But being we're of the weaker sex, we don't get much chance.

ORDERLY: Oh, I'd say you do very well. Very well. (*He goes out.*)

MISS FRAUNCES: You see, Mattie. "They also serve who only stand and wait."

MATTIE: Wait on table . . . is that what it means? (*The outside door is open, and* VAN STARN *stands there, knocking on the door frame. He is a middle-aged farmer.*)

VAN STARN: 'Morning, Miss Fraunces. I've brought the turnips and potatoes you wanted, and some more peas.

MISS FRAUNCES: That's fine, Mr. Van Starn. Put the turnips and potatoes in the root cellar, will you, please? And bring the peas into the kitchen.

VAN STARN: Yes'm. (*Goes*)

MISS FRAUNCES: Now, Mattie, think what a service you can do for your country when you shell more peas for the General!

MATTIE: Fightin' the British with both hands!

MISS FRAUNCES: Cheer up, perhaps you will see that nice young man in the General's Guard again tonight. Then you will forget all your troubles.

MATTIE: Mr. Hickey? (*Bursts out*) Now, that's what I mean, Miss Fraunces. Here's Mr. Hickey, one of General Washington's bodyguard. Think of what *he's* doin' for the war, for the cause of freedom. I mean, compared to shellin' peas.

MISS FRAUNCES: It's a responsible job to be a bodyguard, all right. And a great honor.

MATTIE: Mr. Hickey's proud of it. Though he hasn't come right out and said so. We haven't had much occasion yet to talk of such matters, he being an Irishman with a wag to his tongue in the direction of the ladies.

MISS FRAUNCES: And very handsome, isn't he? (VAN STARN *comes back with a big basket of peas.*)

VAN STARN: Here are the peas, Miss Fraunces. (*Hesitates*) There's . . . a little matter I'd like to take up with you. Mind, I'm not blaming you . . . but it's hard on a poor farmer, money not being worth much at best . . .

MISS FRAUNCES: What is it, Mr. Van Starn? Haven't I been paying you enough?

VAN STARN: Enough, yes. Except that . . .

MISS FRAUNCES: What?

VAN STARN: I go to buy a new bridle at the saddlers, and

what does he tell me? Half the bills you gave me are counterfeit.

MISS FRAUNCES: Counterfeit! How could that be?

VAN STARN: They tell me it's a trick of the British, making counterfeit bills and flooding them around, so the people will lose faith in our paper money. All I know . . . I didn't get the bridle I needed.

MISS FRAUNCES: How dreadful. I'll make it up to you, of course, when I pay you the end of the week.

VAN STARN: Thank you, ma'am. They tell me you never know where these counterfeiters are with their packets of bills to circulate.

MATTIE (*Aside*): Packets of bills!

MISS FRAUNCES: As if we haven't enough troubles trying to finance the war.

VAN STARN: That's just it. (*Turns to go*)

MISS FRAUNCES: Oh, by the way, Mr. Van Starn . . . any time you have more peas, I'd like to buy them. General Washington is very fond of peas.

VAN STARN: Should be more in a day or two. I'll bring them. Good day to you. (*Goes*)

MATTIE: Packets of bills. No, it can't be. Not him!

MISS FRAUNCES: What are you mumbling about, Mattie?

MATTIE: They don't get a very big salary, do they?

MISS FRAUNCES: Who?

MATTIE: The soldiers. I mean, I'm specially thinkin' of the bodyguard.

MISS FRAUNCES: Oh, Mr. Hickey?

MATTIE: What's their pay, Miss Fraunces?

MISS FRAUNCES: I really don't know, Mattie. But it isn't high . . . nor regular, either.

MATTIE: Then he wouldn't have much occasion for packets of bills, would he?

MISS FRAUNCES: What are you trying to get at, Mattie?

MATTIE: You said we had to keep our eyes open, remember? Well, I guess I haven't been keeping mine in the back of my head. But I don't want to be a rabbit jumpin' in the wrong direction either.

MISS FRAUNCES: Go on.

MATTIE: It was when I was cleanin' the guards' room— the one Mr. Hickey and Mr. Green share. The upper drawer of the highboy was a little open, and I couldn't help seein', Miss Fraunces.

MISS FRAUNCES: Seeing what?

MATTIE: The packets of bills. They wouldn't be earning that much, would they?

MISS FRAUNCES: Hardly. Mattie! Maybe we've no right to be suspicious of a likely-looking young man with a wag to his tongue. But this is war. We have to be on the alert. We have to find out, in a quiet way, if Mr. Hickey is the patriot he poses to be. The men are gone now . . . . slip up and get one of the bills from the packet. You can put it back later. No one need ever know.

MATTIE: I can't believe he'd do a thing like that.

MISS FRAUNCES: Neither can I. But we must be sure. It looks queer . . . Run along, Mattie. (MATTIE *hurries out.* MISS FRAUNCES *works around. There is a knock at the inner door.*) Come in!

ORDERLY (*At door*): I forgot to tell you, Miss Fraunces, the General will be having five guests for dinner tonight.

MISS FRAUNCES: I will see to it that the places are set.

ORDERLY (*Seeing the peas*): More peas! You did that in a hurry. Talk about efficiency.

MISS FRAUNCES: We have to thank the good Lord and Van Starn for the peas. Our only contribution is the shelling. Oh, that reminds me, sir. Van Starn says I gave him several counterfeit bills when I paid him last week. Do you know anything about counterfeit bills?

ORDERLY: Too much, unfortunately. The British figure if they can flood the market with counterfeit bills, our money won't be worth the paper it's printed on.

MISS FRAUNCES: Can you tell a counterfeit bill when you see one?

ORDERLY: I think so. I've examined them for the General. He's worried about it, I can tell you.

MISS FRAUNCES: I've just sent Mattie for . . . a bill. I have to keep my housekeeping account straight. Perhaps you can tell me . . . (MATTIE *comes in with bill.*) Here she is now. Show the Orderly the bill, Mattie, so we won't make a mistake again in paying Van Starn.

ORDERLY (*Taking bill, holding it to light*): It has all the earmarks of a counterfeit.

MISS FRAUNCES: Good gracious! Next time I'm going to ask you to be present when I pay the weekly accounts. Folks get little enough for their work without having counterfeit bills to contend with. (*Smiles at* ORDERLY) Guests for dinner tonight . . . and fresh green peas. Mattie can't *wait* to shell those peas.

ORDERLY (*Leaving*): Mattie is a first-class patriot! (*Goes*)

MISS FRAUNCES (*Turning over bill*): I'm afraid that's more than can be said for your Mr. Hickey, Mattie. He's not a man to be trusted.

MATTIE: The beast! Just wait till I see him. I'll do more than wag my tongue!

MISS FRAUNCES: Now, Mattie, control yourself. We must report Mr. Hickey immediately. (*Pause*) No, maybe not. Maybe we should try to find out more of what he is up to first. There's no telling how far a man like that might go.

MATTIE: But how can we find anything out, Miss Fraunces?

MISS FRAUNCES: This may be your chance to do more than keep house for the General!

MATTIE: Mine? (*Excited*) So I won't be just scrubbin' and cleanin', you mean?

MISS FRAUNCES: You and Mr. Hickey are on friendly terms. Perhaps if you lead him to think you are a Tory at heart, he will confide in you. Think hard, Mattie. Have you spoken out your feelings at all about our fight for liberty? Have you told Mr. Hickey how you feel?

MATTIE: Nothin' beyond mentioning I wished *I* could be one of the General's Guard, holdin' an important post like that. Nothin' beyond mentioning I'd like to skin all the Redcoats alive.

MISS FRAUNCES: Mercy! Mr. Hickey would never confide in you! If he's plotting anything, he'd never breathe a word of it into *your* ear. I hoped you might be able to pry something out of him . . . but we'll have to do it some other way. Have you ever mentioned *me* to Mr. Hickey, Mattie?

MATTIE (*Thinking hard*): No, I don't believe I have. No, I'm sure I haven't.

MISS FRAUNCES: Good. Then you must plant the idea this very night that I upset you. You must plant the idea that you think I am with the British at heart . . . that I am opposed to the War. You must say you are afraid that if I get hold of any information here at Mortier House, I'll pass it along to the British. And tell Mr. Hickey to keep your suspicions a secret until you get some real proof.

MATTIE: I'll plant more seeds than in a garden, Miss Fraunces, if you think that will help the cause. But how will it?

MISS FRAUNCES: If Mr. Hickey thinks I am loyal to the King, he will undoubtedly approach me. Then, by playing my cards carefully, I can find out what he has in mind . . . what sort of bodyguard he really is for our great General.

MATTIE: Oh, Miss Fraunces. And here I thought there wasn't any way we could serve except sweepin' and shuckin' peas!

CURTAIN

* * *

SCENE 2

TIME: *Several days later, before dinner.*
SETTING: *Same as Scene 1.*
AT RISE: MISS FRAUNCES *and* MATTIE *are preparing dinner.*

MISS FRAUNCES: To think what a packet of counterfeit bills can lead to, Mattie!

MATTIE: And us in the thick of it. I never was so on edge in my life, Miss Fraunces. (*Beating bowl of batter*) It's a comfort to be beatin' something.

MISS FRAUNCES: You played your part well, planting those seeds about me. Mr. Hickey has been cultivating me for all he is worth.

MATTIE: You should have heard how I dropped them in his ear, innocent as a day-old lamb, you might say. (*Laughs*) And him takin' you for a Tory and tellin' you the whole plot and all!

MISS FRAUNCES: I thank the Lord for that.

MATTIE: If only you'd hear from the General that he got your warning letter, Miss Fraunces.

MISS FRAUNCES: I've been like a cat on hot bricks for the past few hours. Why doesn't he answer? How can I go through with the plot if I don't hear? What if the Orderly forgot to deliver my letter?

MATTIE: Maybe you should have tried to see General Washington yourself, face to face. Maybe.

MISS FRAUNCES: But how could I? With Mr. Hickey in the bodyguard? And goodness knows how many other spies around. No, I couldn't take that chance. I had to write him instead.

MATTIE: You did it real clever-like. No grounds for the Orderly to suspect anything. "A surprise for General Washington," you said.

MISS FRAUNCES: I couldn't come right out and say it was a matter of life and death, Mattie. What if the Orderly is a Tory, too? One can never be sure these days. (*Looks around nervously*) The very walls have ears.

MATTIE: "Something to do with a dinner party," you said. Oh, and what a dinner party! With that dish of green peas in front of the General! "A surprise for the staff, too," you said. No, there couldn't be anything suspicious about that.

MISS FRAUNCES: If General Washington got my warning, why doesn't he send word? I told him I had to be sure. How can we serve the peas to him if we aren't sure, Mattie? How can we?

MATTIE: How can we get out of it, either, without makin' Mr. Hickey suspicious? Oh, but we're in a fix, Miss Fraunces. Up to our very ears.

MISS FRAUNCES (*Nervously*): What are we going to do?

MATTIE: Now, remember what you told me. We women have to keep our hearts strong and our courage up.

MISS FRAUNCES: That was easy to say . . . before we were mixed up in this dreadful plot. Oh, why doesn't the General send an answer?

MATTIE: Just a few words. That's all we need. Just a few words that he won't eat the peas.

MISS FRAUNCES: The whole war depends on what happens tonight. The whole fate of America!

MATTIE (*Excited*): And us in the thick of it, Miss Fraunces! When's Mr. Hickey plannin' to bring the poison?

MISS FRAUNCES: Any time now. I'll have to send you out when he comes.

MATTIE: And it's a good thing or I'd be scratchin' his eyes out. To think that a few days ago I looked on him as the most handsome man in the Army! (*Looks out window*) There he comes now, the traitor. From the stable.

MISS FRAUNCES: Let's be talking commonplaces, in case he comes in without knocking. How did the pound cake turn out?

MATTIE: It fell again in the middle, like a sway-backed horse. It's the oven, I tell you. The recipe says a slow oven, but ours either runs away with itself or dies down entirely. I hope to live to see the day we make a perfect pound cake . . .

HICKEY (*At door*): So do I! Good evening, ladies. (*To* MATTIE) And how is the little Rose of Sharon today?

MATTIE: I'd thank you to be less flowery, sir.

HICKEY: Aren't you the quick one, though? But I like you the better for your spice. Come on, Mattie—how about a nice cool glass of milk to take the edge off my thirst?

MATTIE: And where would I be gettin' a glass of cool milk in a hot kitchen on a June day?

MISS FRAUNCES: Run down to the milk-house and get some, Mattie. We'll need it for dinner, anyway. Take the large pitcher. And mind you don't disturb the crocks we're saving for butter.

HICKEY: And don't run too fast, my little maid, on a June day! (MATTIE *takes pitcher and goes out, giving* HICKEY *a pert look as she passes him.*) We have to hurry! (*Goes to inner door, closes it, locks it*) I brought the Paris green. (*Looks to see that* MATTIE *is really on her way*) Are the peas ready? Where are they? Quick, before Mattie gets back.

MISS FRAUNCES (*Hesitating*): I'm afraid the General is having guests for dinner again tonight. Wouldn't it be better tomorrow?

HICKEY: We can't wait. You aren't backing out on me, are you, Miss Fraunces?

MISS FRAUNCES: Of course not. What a question!

HICKEY: We can't wait because everything's all set. There was a meeting at the tavern again last night. Three hours from now our men will start blowing up the rebel ammunition dumps. The General must be out of the way before that happens. With their ammunition gone and their General gone, the rebel ranks will fall apart like a stack of jackstraws. We'll take over New York City in no time. Hand me the peas . . . (MISS FRAUNCES *fills dish from kettle and brings it to* HICKEY.) That was a stroke of genius, thinking of green peas. (*Stirs in poison*)

MISS FRAUNCES: The General's favorite dish. He can't get enough of them.

HICKEY: Here's one time he'll get enough . . . and to spare. Where can I set this dish to keep it from getting mixed up with the others?

MISS FRAUNCES: Here on the chimney-shelf above the oven. To keep them warm.

HICKEY: We can't take a chance on a rattle-brained girl like Mattie. You must serve the peas to the General yourself. Understand?

MISS FRAUNCES: That I will, with my own hands.

HICKEY: You will be paid well for your part in this, Miss Fraunces.

MISS FRAUNCES (*Trying to be light-hearted*): In counterfeit bills, Mr. Hickey?

HICKEY: No sir-ee. In good British gold. (*Glancing at door*) Here she comes with the milk. (*Changes tone*) . . . that's what I say, too. There's a flavor to pork you don't get in lamb. And as for fowl, give me a piece of roast beef any day.

MATTIE (*Coming in with milk, going to pour glass*): Here's to your health, Mr. Hickey. May it flourish like a garden. (*Gives him glass*)

HICKEY: Mattie, you have a poetic tongue, you have. (*Drinks*)

MATTIE: That's from spendin' my days among the pots and pans, sir.

HICKEY (*Laughs*): And a fortunate thing it is for the likes of me! Well, I must spruce up a bit before dinner. The General always expects his men to put their best foot forward.

MATTIE: Mind you don't trip on yours, Mr. Hickey! (HICKEY, *chuckling, goes out.* MATTIE *watches until it is safe to talk.* MISS FRAUNCES *unlocks inner door.*) Did he do it?

MISS FRAUNCES (*Pointing*): There are the peas, all poisoned. Oh, Mattie, how can I set them before the General not knowing . . . not being sure he won't eat them? It's getting so close to dinner-time, if we don't hear soon . . .

MATTIE: I'm nervous as a hen, I am. Wasn't life simple, though, when we had nothin' but housekeepin' on our minds, Miss Fraunces?

MISS FRAUNCES: And now . . . (*Knock on inner door*) Yes?

ORDERLY (*At door*): The General was interested in your surprise, Miss Fraunces. (*Holds out note*) At least, he asked me to give you this reply. When is the party to come off, may I ask?

MISS FRAUNCES (*Taking the note without a show of emotion*): You'll know soon enough. If I told you, it wouldn't be a surprise, you know. Thank you for bringing the answer. (*She casually puts note in apron pocket.*)

ORDERLY: Always glad to oblige when there's a surprise in the offing. (*Goes*)

MATTIE: Hurry, Miss Fraunces. Read it! Read it! (*She looks to see that the coast is clear.*) I'll keep watch.

MISS FRAUNCES (*Opening letter nervously*): Thank God he got my warning. (*Begins to read*) "My dear Miss Fraunces: I am, I must confess, greatly disturbed by your letter. That such treachery should be afoot in my own bodyguard stuns me. I thank God for the guiding hand that has made itself manifest in your person, and for your quick thinking and acting that will soon bring this matter to a head."

MATTIE: Thomas Hickey's head! Hangin' by a rope!

MISS FRAUNCES (*Reading*): "You must by all means go through with the plot. Only in that way will we have the necessary evidence. Let the dish of green peas be served to me at dinner. I shall not eat them. As soon as the dishes are cleared from the table, have your maid throw most of the peas out to the chickens . . ."

MATTIE: That's me! That's me havin' a hand in it.

MISS FRAUNCES (*Reading*): "Let the balance be kept for evidence. I shall watch from the window and call for an explanation when the chickens die from the poison. You must then, with feigned reluctance, confess that the peas were poisoned, and in your confession implicate Mr. Hickey. And here I must ask your great indulgence, for occasionally great service to one's country must be attended with temporary disgrace."

MATTIE: Temporary disgrace, Miss Fraunces? Does he mean *you?*

MISS FRAUNCES (*Reading*): "You, as well as the traitor, will be thrown in prison . . ."

MATTIE: Prison! Why, that's almost as good as carryin' a gun!

MISS FRAUNCES (*Reading*): "Of course, your imprisonment will be short, for you will be jailed merely as a blind while other members of the plot are rounded up. I have often thought how those who serve in quiet ways are sometimes more our heroes than those for whom the drums roll and the bells toll. Believe me, my dear Miss Fraunces, your grateful friend, George Washington."

MATTIE: Grateful friend . . . (*Sighs ecstatically*)

MISS FRAUNCES: Oh, I'm so relieved, Mattie. And so humble . . . to think we had the privilege of saving the General. Doing what soldiers in the field couldn't do.

MATTIE: And me objectin' to our lot a few days past. Me thinkin' 'twas only men had a chance to serve their country. How right you were, Miss Fraunces. Women don't have to fight to be in the thick of things. They can stay right at home . . . and shell peas!

THE END

Historical Note: Thomas Hickey was the first Revolutionary soldier to be hanged for treachery to the cause.

Yankee Doodle Dandy

Characters

FOUR RECRUITS
OTHER RECRUITS
TWO WOMEN TORIES
TWO MEN TORIES

TIME: *Early in the Revolutionary War*
SETTING: *A street in New York City (which at the time of the Revolution had a population of about 20,000).*
AT RISE: *Young* RECRUITS *are marching down the street. They find it hard to keep in step, and look more like farm boys than soldiers. One has jauntily stuck a feather in his hat.* TORIES *(who side with England) watch from the sidelines and make slighting remarks about the young soldiers.*

1ST RECRUIT: What we need are horses. Then we'd cut a dash.
2ND RECRUIT: A few uniforms wouldn't hurt.
3RD RECRUIT: A marching song—that's what we need. We could keep in step with a good marching song.
1ST WOMAN (*Laughing*): Look at those country bumpkins trying to be soldiers!

107

2ND WOMAN: Aren't they too funny for words!

1ST RECRUIT: Did you hear what she called us? Country bumpkins.

2ND RECRUIT: Don't get your dander up. New York is full of Tories, and they're full of remarks.

1ST RECRUIT: Near as I can figure, all the thirteen colonies are full of Tories.

3RD RECRUIT: John Adams says about a third of the country is on the side of the King. That makes a million people . . .

4TH RECRUIT: Company mark time! One . . . two . . . (RECRUITS *awkwardly mark time near side of stage.*)

1ST WOMAN: That cocky little one with the feather in his hat—isn't he a macaroni, though!

2ND WOMAN: *Isn't* he!

3RD RECRUIT (*Out of corner of mouth*): What's a macaroni?

2ND RECRUIT: They're making fun of us, that's all. Don't pay any attention.

3RD RECRUIT: I know I've got a feather in my hat. But what's a macaroni?

1ST RECRUIT: Just another word for a "dandy," Bud. You know . . . dressed up and fancy.

3RD RECRUIT: Oh. So they're making fun of my feather. (*Sets hat at an even more jaunty angle*) I'll show them.

4TH RECRUIT: Company right about face. March! Hup . . . hup . . . (*The* RECRUITS *aren't very clever carrying out the orders.* TORIES *titter.*)

1ST MAN (*Calling out*): Very clever in the saddle, boys!

2ND MAN: Keep your horses' heads up. Draw in on the reins!

1ST RECRUIT: If I had a horse, or even a pony, I'd show them a thing or two.

2ND RECRUIT: Aw, don't listen to them. If only we had a good marching song, we'd do better. Wouldn't get out of step so much.

1ST MAN (*Jeering*): Let's try a little cantering.

2ND MAN: Cavalry, gallop!

1ST WOMAN: Yankee Doodles from the country. Just out of the hayfields.

4TH RECRUIT: Company halt! Right about face! Mark time!

1ST RECRUIT: Yankee Doodles. Did you hear that? What's a doodle, anyway?

3RD RECRUIT: Just a term of endearment for you and me.

2ND RECRUIT: Doodle? Some term of endearment, since it means "dolt, blockhead, numskull, dullard, dunce, and ignoramus." That's all. That's all they're calling us!

2ND WOMAN: Yankee Doodles. See how they doodle around.

1ST MAN (*Singsong*): Yankee Doodle went to town, a-riding on a pony. (TORIES *laugh.*)

1ST WOMAN (*Picking up the singsong*): He stuck a feather in his cap, and . . . and called it macaroni! (*Laughter*)

2ND WOMAN: Why, that's a little poem. You've made a poem about the country clowns. (*Chants*) Yankee Doodle went to town, a-riding on his pony. He stuck a feather in his cap, and called it macaroni.

4TH RECRUIT (*Eagerly*): That's got swing, boys! Sounds like something to march to! Let's throw it back at them, boys. Heads up! Chins in! Eyes front! Let's show them what we've got. Right about face . . . company march! "Yankee Doodle went to town . . .

RECRUITS (*Joining in, keeping time to rhythm*):

"A-riding on a pony,
He stuck a feather in his cap,
And called it macaroni."

(*Voices up spontaneously*)
Yankee Doodle keep it up,
Yankee Doodle, dandy,
Mind the music and the step
And with the girls be handy!

(*They march out*)

1ST WOMAN: My goodness, did you hear that? The idea caught on for a marching song.

2ND WOMAN: It certainly did.

1ST MAN: Well, what do you think of that! They didn't even know we were making fun of them! Didn't even know we were poking fun at their expense.

2ND WOMAN: Either they didn't know . . . or they're not such doodles, after all. (RECRUITS *come marching back like veterans, singing another stanza of "Yankee Doodle."*)

4TH RECRUIT: Company halt! Doff your hats to the Tories . . . one . . . two . . .

RECRUITS (*Bowing deeply*): Yankee Doodle dandies!

THE END

NOTE: The origin of "Yankee Doodle" is uncertain. Several sources point out the probability that it was first used by the British in derision of the colonial soldiers, and that it was later adopted by the Americans as their favorite marching song. Other commentators think the words too "gentle" for derision. The tune was known in the colonies as early as 1767.

Ask Mr. Jefferson

Characters

PHIL
SHERRY
CLARK
DONNA
THOMAS JEFFERSON

SCENE 1

SETTING: *The first short scene takes place in front of the curtain.* PHIL, SHERRY, CLARK *and* DONNA, *with note-books and pencils, seem rather perplexed.*

PHIL: Interview him in the library, Miss Whitney said.
SHERRY: I guess that's about the only place we *could* interview him in this day and age. He'll come alive for us there.
PHIL: I bet he's an old fogy. Out of date. Stuffy.
DONNA: I don't know about that, Phil. Abraham Lincoln said that Jefferson's principles are the definitions of a free society.
CLARK: What's a free society?
DONNA: A democracy. The United States of America!
CLARK: Where'd you get all that, Donna?
DONNA: I've been to the library before!

PHIL: Well, we're going to have to change the name of the report, that's for sure, or no one in class will listen. JEFFERSON'S IDEAS OF DEMOCRACY AS APPLIED TO MODERN AMERICA. Can you imagine holding anyone's attention with that?

CLARK (*Shrugging*): What's the alternative?

SHERRY: We'd better all keep the problem of a title in mind during the interview. We need something snappy. Something catchy. There's only one rule Miss Whitney laid down, remember. She doesn't want us to make anything up. She wants us to quote Jefferson word for word.

CLARK: Verbatim.

PHIL: O.K. Let's get it over with. (*They exit.*)

* * *

SCENE 2

SETTING: *A library.*

AT RISE: THOMAS JEFFERSON *is seated at one of the tables, with books, manuscripts, letters around him. He is looking through some papers when the four interviewers enter.*

SHERRY (*To* PHIL): Miss Whitney was right. There he is!

PHIL: How do you know?

SHERRY: I've seen pictures. So have you, Phil.

PHIL: All those old fellows look alike to me. Except Washington. (*They stand wondering what to do.*)

CLARK: How do we go about it? Where do we start? What do we say?

DONNA: Why don't we just lay the facts on the table— tell him why we're here, and begin to ask him some questions about rights and freedom and that sort of thing?

PHIL: You start, Donna. You've been to the library before! (*They approach* MR. JEFFERSON.)

DONNA (*Sweetly*): Pardon me, Mr. Jefferson. Would you be so kind as to answer a few questions? You see, we have to give a report to the class about your ideas of democracy and . . .

PHIL: Frankly, we're not too sure of our ground.

DONNA: We want to quote you *directly*, so there won't be any doubt about what you believe. Clark, you ask Mr. Jefferson the first question. You're good at asking questions.

CLARK (*Hesitating*): Not in a library. Well . . . well, do you believe in liberty, sir?

JEFFERSON (*Slowly, in measured tones*): "The God who gave us life, gave us liberty at the same time."

CLARK (*Surprised, to* DONNA): What do you know! He had the answer on the tip of his tongue. (*Interviewers take notes throughout.* JEFFERSON *speaks slowly and impressively.*)

SHERRY: I think we ought to organize our interview a little, so we won't take too much of Mr. Jefferson's time.

PHIL: Not to mention ours.

DONNA: Let's ask him about rights. That's one of the big things in a democracy. (*To* JEFFERSON) You believe that men are born with certain rights that can't be taken away from them, don't you?

JEFFERSON: "Certain unalienable rights."

DONNA: Just what rights do you mean, Mr. Jefferson?

JEFFERSON: "Among these are life, liberty, and the pursuit

of happiness. . . . To secure these rights governments are instituted among men."

PHIL: You mean it's up to a *government* to see that everyone has freedom and happiness?

JEFFERSON: "The freedom and happiness of man . . . are the sole objects of all legitimate government."

PHIL (*Taking notes*): Gosh, that's good. That's where dictators go wrong, see? They want freedom for themselves, but they want the people to take orders. We're lucky in the United States, I tell you. Say, Mr. Jefferson, do you believe our idea of freedom and happiness for everyone is going to spread . . . around the world maybe?

JEFFERSON: "This ball of liberty, I believe most piously, is now so well in motion that it will roll round the globe, at least the enlightened part of it, for light and liberty go together."

CLARK: Not so fast, sir. Would you mind repeating the end of that again?

JEFFERSON: . . . "light and liberty go together."

PHIL: This is hot stuff.

DONNA (*To* PHIL): Coming from an old fogy! (*To* JEFFERSON) You believe in equality, don't you, Mr. Jefferson?

JEFFERSON: "All men are created equal."

SHERRY: Equal in rights and opportunity. And that means the government should be in the hands of all men, not just the rich . . . isn't that true, sir?

CLARK: Don't put words in his mouth, Sherry!

JEFFERSON: "I am not among those who fear the people. They, and not the rich, are our dependence for continued freedom."

PHIL: Check!

DONNA: But how can people, just *any* kind of people, be trusted with running the government, Mr. Jefferson? They at least have to have an education, don't they?

CLARK: Of course, they do. That's taken for granted.

SHERRY: Now who's putting words in his mouth?

JEFFERSON: "No one more sincerely wishes the spread of information among mankind than I do, and none has greater confidence in its effect towards supporting free and good government."

PHIL: Say, Mr. Jefferson, you're right up to date!

SHERRY: You mean, when voters keep up on what's happening, and know what they're voting for, there's nothing to worry about. Is that it, Mr. Jefferson?

JEFFERSON: "Whenever the people are well-informed, they can be trusted with their own government: whenever things get so far wrong as to attract their notice, they may be relied on to set them to rights."

CLARK (*Looking up from notebook*): Sometimes it takes people an awful long time to wake up to what is wrong, though.

PHIL: But trusting the common sense of the people is a surer way to freedom and happiness than trusting a dictator. Isn't that right, Mr. Jefferson?

JEFFERSON: "The way to have a good and safe government is not to trust it all to one, but to divide it among the many. . . . I would rather be exposed to the inconveniences attending too much liberty, than those attending too small a degree of it."

PHIL: Me, too. And nobody's ever going to brain-wash me out of it. (*Suddenly*) Say, let's ask Mr. Jefferson what he thinks of brain-washing.

CLARK: He never even heard of it.

SHERRY: Not in those words, anyway.

DONNA: Put it in terms of the Bill of Rights, Phil, and he'll know what you're talking about. You know, ask him about freedom of speech and all that.

PHIL: What do you think about our right to say what we want, and worship the way we please, and think our own thoughts, sir?

JEFFERSON: "There are rights which it is useless to surrender to the government, and which governments have yet always been found to invade. These are the rights of thinking, and publishing our thoughts by speaking or writing. . . . I have sworn upon the altar of God hostility against every form of tyranny over the mind of man."

PHIL (*Excited*): Wait a minute! That sounds like the lead sentence in our report. Mr. Jefferson, you've got all the answers! Would you mind repeating that last sentence again, sir?

JEFFERSON: "I have sworn upon the altar of God hostility against every form of tyranny over the mind of man."

SHERRY (*Who has been taking notes industriously, looking up*): Say, I've thought of the perfect, catchy title for our report. Phil, you gave me the idea just now.

PHIL: Me?

SHERRY: You said Mr. Jefferson had all the answers. And it's true. He's got the answers for our day as well as his. All we have to do is ask him. The way we've been doing.

PHIL: So what?

SHERRY: So let's call our report, "Ask Mr. Jefferson."

CLARK: That'll catch attention, all right. What do you think, Mr. Jefferson?

JEFFERSON (*Smiling a little roguishly*): "I tolerate with

the utmost latitude the right of others to differ from me in opinion."

SHERRY (*Laughing*): You see, he's got all the answers—on the tip of his tongue.

DONNA (*Showing paper*): Look, I've written a little verse. Maybe we could start our report with it and go on from there. (*Reads*)

> He spoke for freedom years ago—
> His vision still is clear today,
> His words still guide us as we go
> Along the democratic way . . .

OTHERS: Ask Mr. Jefferson!

THE END

"Molly Pitcher"

Characters

1ST SOLDIER
2ND SOLDIER
3RD SOLDIER
MOLLY
SOLDIERS, *any number, without speaking parts*

TIME: *Afternoon of a blistering hot day, June 28, 1778.*
SETTING: *Part of an orchard within sight of the Monmouth Court House, in New Jersey, where an important battle is taking place (the Battle of Monmouth) between the patriots and the Redcoats.*
AT RISE: *Patriot* SOLDIERS *in tattered shirts cross stage, crouching, aiming at enemy, moving ahead. They are obviously tired and hot, on the point of exhaustion.* 1ST SOLDIER *and* 2ND SOLDIER *stumble in, fall behind tree. For a moment they lie there gasping, as other* SOLDIERS *pass.*

1ST SOLDIER:
    All winter at Valley Forge we shivered,
    Froze our fingers, and quaked and quivered . . .
2ND SOLDIER:
    All winter we froze from lack of shelter

118

And lack of clothing . . . and now we swelter!

1ST SOLDIER:

It's over a hundred in the shade.
My tongue feels big as a garden spade,
And my ears are split from the cannonade.

2ND SOLDIER:

Heat and dust and noise and slaughter—
And all I ask is a drink of water!

1ST SOLDIER (*Moaning*): Water!

2ND SOLDIER (*Moaning*): Water!

For days we've followed the British wagons
Winding north like a chain of dragons,
And when we're up to the foe at last . . .
Most of my strength to fight has passed! (*Sighs*)

1ST SOLDIER:

At least, we're lucky we're not as warm
As men in a Redcoat uniform.
You noticed them strewn along the way—
More struck by the sun than by guns today.
(*With an effort he raises his head, peeks over log, then takes aim, shoots, and draws back.*)
One Redcoat less to enjoy the weather,
The sun, the dust, and the thirst together!

2ND SOLDIER (*Trying to sit up, but falling back again*):

My tongue's so taut it could not be tauter.
Oh, for a drink of good cool water.

1ST SOLDIER: Water!

2ND SOLDIER: Water! (*They lie back exhausted as more SOLDIERS pass. 3RD SOLDIER stops, looks, leans over.*)

3RD SOLDIER:

Boys, can you hear? Then listen to me:
There's a right good chance for a victory.
We're pressing Clinton at every quarter!

2ND SOLDIER (*Moaning*):
 What we need is a drink of water.
3RD SOLDIER:
 You know what the Redcoats call us? "Herdsmen!
 Farmers! Bumpkins!" Their very words, men.
 Show them they've made a grievous error,
 Show them we'll push them back in terror!
1ST SOLDIER (*Trying to get up*):
 The spirit's willing. The flesh is weak.
 My tongue's so thick I can hardly speak.
2ND SOLDIER: A drink of water is all we seek! (*He tries
 to rise, staggers. 3RD SOLDIER catches him, puts him
 down again.*)
3RD SOLDIER (*Looking around*):
 Where's that Molly? She'll fix you up.
 She's got a pitcher and drinking cup.
1ST SOLDIER:
 A pitcher and drinking cup sounds jolly,
 But who in the name of the war is Molly?
3RD SOLDIER:
 Molly's a lass we all can praise—
 Her name's McCauley, though some say Hayes,
 And some say Heis, and a few, McGuire—
 You can choose the one that you most admire.
 Whatever her name, it doesn't matter,
 As long as Molly has cheer to scatter
 And water to pass in a pewter cup . . .
1ST SOLDIER AND 2ND SOLDIER: Find her, oh, find her, and
 hurry up! (*3RD SOLDIER hurries out.*)
1ST SOLDIER:
 A lass in the midst of noise and slaughter,
 Passing out drinks of precious water?

2ND SOLDIER:

    A lass in the midst of pain and danger,

    Quenching the thirst of friend and stranger?

1ST SOLDIER:

    Since no one's certain which name is whicher,

    Why don't we christen her Molly *Pitcher* . . .

    Molly Pitcher, with pitcher and cup,

    Helping to bolster our spirits up!

(3RD SOLDIER *returns with* MOLLY, *points at* 1ST SOLDIER
and 2ND.)

3RD SOLDIER:

    Those two, Molly. They're quite done in,

    And we need all hands if we're going to win. (*He nods
goodbye and hurries out.*)

1ST SOLDIER (*As* MOLLY *pours water*):

    To me you look like an angel's daughter,

    Bringing a drink of saving water.

MOLLY (*Laughing*):

    No angel's daughter . . . a gunner's wife,

    Who wants to help in this noble strife!

    Liberty, boys, is a prized possession.

    Down with the Briton, down with the Hessian!

    (*Hands* 1ST SOLDIER *cup of water*)

    Take it easy . . . then rest a minute.

    (*Takes cup from* 1ST SOLDIER, *fills it, hands it to* 2ND SOL-
DIER):

    Savor each sip and swallow in it!

1ST SOLDIER:

    A gunner's wife in the midst of battle

    Where cannons roar and where sabers rattle!

MOLLY (*Pointing*):

    My husband's cannon is over there.

    See? By the tree on the Court House square.

1ST SOLDIER:
Firing in all this heat, I swear.
MOLLY: Another drink? (*Pours more water*): Then I must
be moving.
I hope your spirits will be improving.
My husband's certain that we can win
If we *stick to our guns* through thick and thin.
(*She looks toward Court House square . . . then suddenly gasps.*)
Oh! He's wounded! His arm seems broken!
His arm hangs limp, but his heart is oaken.
(*Puts down pitcher, calls out, as she runs offstage*)
I'm coming . . . I'm coming! We can't stop firing!
1ST SOLDIER (*Looking after her*):
Molly Pitcher, the lass inspiring!
She gives me courage, she gives me spirit.
She runs toward the cannon. She's getting near it!
Remember, she said that we can win
If we stick to our guns through thick and thin.
(*He grasps his gun.*)
2ND SOLDIER (*Watching* MOLLY):
Molly Pitcher is quite a runner.
She's reached the cannon, she's reached the gunner.
1ST SOLDIER:
She's loading the cannon. She's ready to fire!
That's the spirit that I admire.
(*He jumps up, full of eagerness, turns and beckons to*
SOLDIERS *to come ahead, shouts encouragement.*)
Liberty, boys, is a prized possession.
Down with the Briton, down with the Hessian!
2ND SOLDIER (*Jumping up, grasping gun*):
Freedom is surer, faith is richer,
After our meeting with Molly Pitcher.

1ST SOLDIER:

    Forward! Forward! We're just beginning

    To rout the British—their ranks are thinning.

BOTH:

    Freedom's ahead, and it's ours for winning!

(As they hurry ahead, other SOLDIERS *follow with spirit.)*

THE END

Freedom in a Word

Characters

TEACHER
JOHNNY
LINDA
RALPH
SEVEN BOYS AND GIRLS

AT RISE: *The seven* BOYS *and* GIRLS *are on stage with cardboard letters behind their backs spelling out F-R-E-E-D-O-M.*

TEACHER (*Nodding to* JOHNNY *in audience*): What is freedom?

JOHNNY:
I don't know . . .
I guess the right to come and go
And speak my mind. I wonder, though.

TEACHER (*Nodding to* LINDA *in audience*): What is freedom?

LINDA:
I'm not sure . . .
I think it means to feel secure
No matter if you're rich or poor.

TEACHER (*Nodding to* RALPH *in audience*): What is freedom?

RALPH: Seems to me
It means the right to disagree
And do a lot of things . . . for free.

TEACHER (*Looking around room*): What is freedom?
Who, oh, who
Knows its meaning through and through?

BOYS AND GIRLS (*On stage*):
We can spell it out for you!

TEACHER (*Surprised*):
Can you? Will you? Come, please do.
(BOYS *and* GIRLS *step forward in turn as they speak
their lines and show their letters on cards.*)

F: F for the future—freedom to hold it
Safe from a tyrant seeking to mold it.

R: R for religion—freedom in choosing
The church and the doctrine we wish to be using.

E: E for being equal—freedom of action
In making our way to our own satisfaction.

E: E—education!—freedom of learning,
Thinking, inquiring, believing, discerning.

D: D for discussion—freedom in speaking
What we believe without cringing and creaking.

O: O—occupation!—freedom to choose it,
Freedom to keep it, change it, or lose it.

M: M for materials—money to earn them,
Freedom to buy them, freedom to spurn them.

BOYS AND GIRLS (*Holding letters high*):
What is freedom all about?
Now you need no longer doubt,
Since we've spelled the whole thing out.

TEACHER (*Nodding*):
Yes, from all that we have heard
That is freedom—in a word!

How to Spell a Patriot

Characters

Boys *and* Girls *(Sixteen)*

Setting: *Across the front of the stage is a chalk line with places marked with letters, in order, spelling* George Washington, *where* Boys *and* Girls *will stand when they say their lines.*

At Rise: Boys *and* Girls *are at back of stage in small groups. Each carries one of the letters that spells out* G-E-O-R-G-E W-A-S-H-I-N-G-T-O-N. *In the beginning the letters are all mixed up. Each child leaves the group and stands on the letter indicated to say his lines.*

Group:
  We can spell a patriot!
  We needn't ask our betters.
  We can spell a patriot
  By using sixteen letters!
H: Take H to stand for honor
  In peace as well as war,
W: Take W for wisdom
  And watchfulness, what's more.
G: Take G to stand for greatness
  In planning and in deed,

G: Take G for goodness also,
    Which even heroes need!
O: Take O for optimism
    When fortune seems to frown,
R: Take R for real resistance
    When trouble presses down.
 I: Take I to stand for insight
    In doing what is best,
 S: Take S for strength in service
    To meet the grimmest test.
T: Take T to stand for talent,
    And also truth and trust,
O: Take O for opposition
    To everything unjust.
N: Take N for noble nature—
    Not seeking fame or power,
 E: Take E for great endurance
    In every crucial hour.
N: Take N for nerve to tackle
    Whatever must be done,
 E: Take E for extra effort
    When battles must be won.
A: Take A for ardent action
    To make injustice cease,
G: Take G to stand for guidance
    In war as well as peace.
ALL (*Holding letters high*):
    There, we spelled a patriot
    In letters big and tall—
    A patriot, GEORGE WASHINGTON,
    The greatest of them all!

The Many Rides of Paul Revere

NARRATOR:
>Listen, my children, and you shall hear
>of the *many* rides of Paul Revere,
>the silversmith whose horse's feet
>pounded many a road and street
>in days when the colonists had cause
>to chafe and fret under British laws.

CHILDREN:
>You mean to say that the midnight ride
>over the April countryside
>in seventeen hundred and seventy-five
>wasn't the *only* ride he took?
>It's famous in every history book.

NARRATOR:
>On *many* a night or noon or morning
>he rode to carry some news or warning.

>Listen, my children, in seventy-three
>Paul Revere helped dump the tea
>from British ships into Boston's port.
>In a patriotic attempt to thwart

the British passion to levy taxes,
the colonists swung their battleaxes!

Then Paul Revere and his trusty horse
carried the news along a course
more than two hundred miles in length,
in winter. It needed a man of strength.
He reached New York with the news to share
with Sons of Liberty active there.

CHILDREN:
All those miles in wintry weather
to bind the patriots together!

NARRATOR:
That isn't all ... it's just the start.
Paul Revere played a worthy part
in getting relief for Boston town
when, early in spring, the British crown
as punishment closed the harbor down.
Off to New York he rode again.
enlisting the help of fellowmen;
then on to Independence Hall
in Philadelphia, to call
upon the patriots there to heed
Boston's plight in its time of need.

CHILDREN:
He covered many a mile indeed.
And did he travel again before
the shot was fired that sparked the war
in seventy-five?

NARRATOR:

> Through seventy-four
> he went on missions again and again
> with news for freedom-devoted men ...
> all for the sake of the cause, of course —
> a middle-aged man on a sturdy horse.
> He won a certain amount of fame:
> "official courier" he became.
> Even the British knew his name.

CHILDREN:

> Then came the time he spread the warning
> in the early hours of an April morning!

NARRATOR:

> He watched to see what the light would be
> in the belfry tower that crucial night:
> one, if by land; two, if by sea.
> He saw two lanterns burning bright,
> and off he sped to cry the alarm
> to every Middlesex village and farm.

CHILDREN:

> "The British are coming! They're on the way."

NARRATOR:

> The war for freedom began that day.
>
> The war for freedom! The call was clear.
> Patriots fought for many a year
> and, thanks to stalwarts like Paul Revere,
> we won the freedom we hold so dear.

The Red, White, and Blue

1.

BOYS: What does it stand for—
The Red, White, and Blue?
GIRLS: It stands for our country
And what it went through
To win us our freedom
When freedom was new.

2.

BOYS: What do they stand for—
The stripes, red and white?
GIRLS: The states on the seaboard
That braved England's might,
Thirteen in number,
United to fight.

3.

BOYS: What do they stand for—
The stars, one and all?
GIRLS: The States in the Union,
The big states and small,
Ready to answer
America's call.

131

4.

Boys: What do they stand for—
The colors we see?
Girls: Red stands for courage,
And white—liberty,
And blue for the staunch
In this land of the free.

5.

All: Hail to our banner
Still shining like new,
Symbol of faith
In the brave and the true,
Symbol of freedom . . .
The Red, White, and Blue!

Who Is It?

Characters

BETTY
BRUCE
BOYS AND GIRLS (twelve)

SETTING: *There is a big "History Book" toward the back of the stage. Only the covers show, and they can be made of screens that will open. It can be very simple. Twelve* BOYS *and* GIRLS *are behind the "Book."* BETTY, *dressed in colonial costume, is at one side of the stage;* BRUCE, *in modern clothes, at the other side.*

BETTY: There was a man in our town
     And he was wondrous wise:
     He did so many helpful things
     His neighbors rubbed their eyes.

BRUCE: Who was the man in your town
     Who was so wondrous wise?
     I wouldn't think that *one* man
     Could make you rub your eyes!

BETTY: He didn't act like one man,
     He acted more like ten,
     And everybody called him
     "Our Leading Citizen."

BRUCE: What was his name and station?
How long ago and when?
What did he do that made him
Your Leading Citizen?

BETTY: Oh, everybody knows him!
Why don't you guess his name?

BRUCE: All right . . . if you will give me
Some hints about his fame.

(BETTY *runs to "History Book" and opens covers.* BOYS *and* GIRLS *come out one by one, as they speak their lines.*)

1ST: He was the first man to propose a union of the thirteen colonies, way back in 1754.

2ND: He started the first public library in America.

3RD: He helped found the first hospital in Philadelphia, and persuaded the people to light the streets, and have them swept.

4TH: He organized the first fire insurance company and a volunteer fire department.

5TH: As Postmaster-general of the colonies, he improved the service so mail was delivered more quickly.

6TH: He wrote and published a famous Almanac, in which he said: "Little strokes fell great oaks."

1ST: "He that goes a borrowing goes a sorrowing."

2ND: "Plough deep while sluggards sleep;
And you shall have corn to sell and to reap."

3RD: "Early to bed and early to rise,
Makes a man healthy, wealthy, and wise."

4TH: "Never leave that till to-morrow which you can do today."

5TH: "Vessels large may venture more,
But little boats should keep near shore."

7TH: He invented a new kind of stove which became

very famous because it didn't waste heat like a fireplace.

8TH: He held many public offices, and went to England to try to get Parliament to give the colonies their rights.

9TH: He helped to frame the Declaration of Independence and the Constitution of the United States, and signed them both.

10TH: He persuaded France to send us ships and soldiers and supplies in our fight for freedom.

11TH: He arranged the Treaty of Peace with England after the Revolutionary War.

12TH: By using a kite with a key on the end of the string, he discovered that there was electricity in lightning . . .

BRUCE: Benjamin Franklin!

ALL: Benjamin Franklin!
He didn't act like one man,
He acted more like ten,
No wonder people called him
Our Leading Citizen!

Bunker Hill

(June, 1775)

Up the hill the British came,
Their red coats flashing in the sun,
As flashing bright as freedom's flame
That fired our soldiers, every one.

Up the hill, three thousand strong,
The British marched to seize the height
Our men had strengthened all night long
In preparation for the fight.

Up the hill, our men's supply
Of powder was distressing small,
And then, at last, the battle cry!
Our volley struck the marching wall.

Redcoats fell and Redcoats ran.
Our farmer-soldiers watched them go,
And nodded grimly, man to man.
Confusion filled the field below.

A second charge! The British still
Outnumbered rebels two to one.

A second volley! Down the hill
The Redcoats ran as madmen run.

Behind the ramparts, powder gone,
Our soldiers waited, tense and true,
They had been fighting since the dawn,
They had been trenching all night through.

Would General Howe resume the fight?
The hill was soaked with British blood,
And then, the unexpected sight—
On came another British flood!

Our men had gunstocks, little more,
So Redcoats won the hill that day.
But, losing what they battled for,
Our soldiers won another way:

They won respect for standing firm,
They won recruits for liberty,
They won what patriots could term
A sort of splendid victory!

Washington at Valley Forge

(December, 1777)

ALL: A wooded valley and a frozen creek,
the hills surrounding, high and cold and bleak;
a little forge for melting metal down,
a valley forge—the kernel of a town,
a dreary place with Christmastime so near . . .

1ST BOY: The General called a halt: "We're camping here.
We'll need some huts as shelter from the cold.
Work quickly, men, the year is growing old."

ALL: The General watched his soldiers chop and saw.
Their feet were bleeding and their hands were raw.
They lacked supplies and clothes and shoes and
food,
but, like their leader, they had fortitude.

2ND BOY: The General stood upon a rise of ground.
His heart was heavy as he looked around:
"My unpaid men are weary, hungry, cold,
while twenty miles away the Redcoats hold
fair Philadelphia and live in state,
and sit in comfort near a blazing grate!

The snow at Valley Forge is stained with red.
My soldiers dream of boots and gloves and bread."

ALL: The General thought of home—Mount Vernon's
         charm.
         His soldiers wintered, what would be the harm
         in going home? The cold had months to run!
         He turned and looked into the puny sun,
         and chose the hardship—as he'd always done—
         the General by the name of Washington.

The Ragged Continentals

They knew full well what must be done,
they knew where freedom's pathway lay,
and so they shouldered pack and gun,
and waved goodbye, and marched away
through rain and mud and snow and sun
to fight to win a better day.

They left their farms, their shops, their wives,
and skirmished with the enemy,
prepared to settle with their lives,
aware that freedom was not free.
They won ... and what they won survives:
that priceless gift of liberty.

My Bet on the Declaration

I've got a brother in college. He's studying law, and I mean studying, putting in long hours and all that. According to him I waste too much time on comics and cowboy stories when I ought to be reading history. The other night I was buried in a Western and he pulled it away from me and bet me a dollar about something. I was mad about losing my book but I took him up on that bet before he had a chance to change his mind. It was something about the Declaration of Independence—the men who signed it, I mean. You see I was to imagine myself back there in 1776 and pick out one signer of the Declaration I would rather have been than any other. My brother bet he could guess the signer I'd pick—and if he didn't guess right, he'd pay me a dollar. Of course, I couldn't pick out one whose only claim to fame was that he signed the Declaration. There had to be some logic behind my choice. Leave it to a law student to talk about logic!

I went at it tooth and nail. After all, dollars don't grow on any bushes I know of. The first name I thought·of choosing was George Washington. Maybe because I knew most about him, the courage he had, and the way he kept on fighting when he had next to nothing to fight with. Then I decided I'd better look up the signers, and I discovered that George Washington didn't sign the

Declaration of Independence at all. If I'd used my head I'd have known that, because he wasn't in Congress in 1776 but off in camp training the army to fight.

What about Benjamin Franklin, I thought? I always liked him, the way he kept experimenting and inventing things. Besides, he was on the Committee appointed by Congress to draw up the Declaration. Not only that, but he was sent to England to protest in Parliament against the tyranny and injustice that made the colonies want to be independent. Then I figured out that Franklin was seventy years old in 1776. Too old for me to want to be Franklin, I decided, so I passed him by.

Next I thought about Thomas Jefferson. He was only thirty-three at the time, and I wouldn't mind looking like him—over six feet tall and with a good shock of red hair. The other four men on the Committee had him draw up the Declaration, and he worked so hard at it that he had a first draft written in two days. "All men are created equal," he wrote. By that he didn't mean that we're all alike. What he meant was that we all ought to be treated alike. He believed in fair play, and so do I. So I'm for him and for what he wrote about everybody having a right to "life, liberty, and the pursuit of happiness." And I'm for government by the people and not by tyrants. Everybody ought to be for that when they see how the Communists, the modern tyrants, rule with an iron hand and make people afraid to call their souls their own. I had just about decided to pick Jefferson, when I realized that I wouldn't know how to act if I was as brainy as he was. I wouldn't feel like myself at all!

That was the trouble with Samuel Adams and with John Adams too. They liked studying too much to suit me. They went to Harvard and practiced law. And I couldn't imagine myself doing that when I want to be a cowboy and ride horses more than anything else. So I looked at the signers again. There was Robert Morris. I remembered hearing my brother call him a financial wizard one time. Morris saved our young republic from bankruptcy, I guess. But then I'm no financier. I always run behind trying to make my allowance stretch, so I decided Robert Morris wasn't for me.

And then my eye lit on the name of Caesar Rodney and I remembered something I'd read about him one time. Something about a horse—a horse! That was my man. He could ride like the wind, and so could I if I had a horse! So I went and looked him up at the library— and say, it was as good as a thriller any day. What happened was this. Caesar Rodney should have been in Philadelphia in his seat as a delegate to the Continental Congress from Delaware. But instead he was back home in the thick of things leading his band of militiamen to southern Delaware to put down a Tory uprising there. He didn't have any use for Tories because they sided with the British instead of helping the cause of freedom. And this time he was more put out with them than usual because he knew he was missing out on the hot argument in Congress for independence.

Then like a bolt from the blue an express rider dashed up with a message from Congress. Rodney tore it open and discovered that his vote was needed to swing Delaware into line for independence. Otherwise Delaware would be the one colony standing out against the break with England and that would never do. There had to be a united front for freedom or the cause would suffer.

I'd give a lot to have been in Rodney's boots at that minute. Not that I'd care to look like him. He was the

oddest looking man in the world according to John
Adams, tall and thin (I wouldn't mind that), with a face
no bigger than an apple. But there was sense and fire and
humor in it, and he needed all three in this crisis. Another man might have decided not to bestir himself since
the Declaration would be adopted anyway even if one
colony dissented. But Rodney wasn't looking for an excuse. He wanted to deliver. Once he knew he was needed
in Philadelphia, he never hesitated a minute. He felt it
was up to him to have Delaware counted on the side of
freedom. So if it was the last thing he did, he'd ride
those eighty miles and get there in time to cast his vote.
He galloped all night, drenched by thunder storms, stopping only long enough to change horses in the rain. Dig-
ging his spurs into each fresh horse, on he went with
only one thought in mind: to get there in time. And he
did. Spattered with mud from head to foot, he dashed up
to the State House in Philadelphia in the nick of time to
cast the vote that made Delaware go down in history on
the side of independence.

Rodney was the man who made it possible for the
Declaration to be adopted without a single colony dissent-
ing. And then later, when it came to the actual signing of
the parchment copy of the Declaration, the one now in
the National Archives, Caesar Rodney signed his name
with a flourish. He knew only too well it would mean a
traitor's death if England won the war, but he was proud
to take that chance.

Yes, there was no doubt of it, Caesar Rodney was my
man. And there was no doubt that I'd have to do something to throw my brother off the track. If he happened
to remember that mad ride of Rodney's, I'd never win
that bet. So I began to ask him a lot of questions about

some of the other signers, and particularly about John Adams, his special favorite. And what did he do but dish a fat copy of a life of Adams on me and tell me to read it. Every time he was around, I'd dip into it and seem interested. And the ruse worked. He guessed that Adams was my man! Imagine! My brother may turn out to be a good enough lawyer, but he'd make a punk detective, not to know that I'd gallop through the night to win that bet.

The Carved Symbol

1ST SOLO: Let's go to Philadelphia,
               To Independence Hall —

2ND SOLO: To see a chair, a stately chair
               (Not over-large, or small)

3RD SOLO: Behind a certain table there,
               Before a certain wall.

4TH SOLO: The head-rest of that high-backed chair
               Is carved with half a sun,
               With many short projecting rays
               In woodwork finely done;

ALL: And for its role in history
               That chair gives place to none.

1ST SOLO: Let's take a journey back in time
               To when that chair was new;
               George Washington presided there
               One fiery summer through
               When delegates from thirteen states
               Had urgent work to do.

2ND SOLO: The War for liberty was won,
               The peace with Britain signed,
               But problems of the thirteen states
               Had not been left behind:

ALL: The pressing need for unity,
            A tie to build and bind.
3RD SOLO: The delegates could not agree
            And tension filled the air
            As bitter words and bickerings
            Were bantered here and there.
            The chairman, Washington, was grave
            Upon his high-backed chair.
4TH SOLO: The months went by, and still no plan
            To which the states agreed.
ALL: Then Franklin said,
FRANKLIN: A government
            For *all* is what we need.
            Let's give and take. Let's compromise.
            Come, gentlemen, proceed.
1ST SOLO: At last the quarrels were compromised
            Between states big and small,
2ND SOLO: Those wanting central power and strength
            Or little strength at all;
3RD SOLO: The Constitution then was signed
            In Independence Hall.
4TH SOLO: When Franklin rose again to speak,
            He pointed to the chair
            Where Washington had sat so long
            With tension in the air,
ALL: And Franklin said,
FRANKLIN: You see that sun,
            That symbol showing there?
            I often wondered if it stood
            For freedom lost, or won.
            I wondered if it set, or rose,
            But now this deed is done

I'm certain of that sun at last —
It is a *rising* one.

ALL: The others cheered,

1ST and 2ND SOLOS: A rising sun
For our democracy!

3RD and 4TH SOLOS: A sun to light the way for us
And for posterity...

ALL: And may it never, never set
Upon our liberty!

His Name Was Nathan Hale

A youthful teacher, slim and tall,
A college boy from Yale,
Gave up his books, his post, his all,
To follow freedom's trail.
    His name was Nathan Hale.

When war broke out in '75
He labored tooth and nail
To help make liberty survive
And despotism fail.
    His name was Nathan Hale.

Next year, he volunteered to go
And find out in detail
The British strength, so we might know
If an attack would fail.
    His name was Nathan Hale.

The youthful soldier, in disguise,
Turned spy to no avail . . .
The British caught him by surprise.
A hanging not a jail!
    His name was Nathan Hale.

He said: I know I shall not live.
What hurts is not to fail,
But having just *one* life to give
So freedom may prevail.
His name was Nathan Hale.

The Liberty Bell Speaks

ALL: "Proclaim liberty throughout all the land and
           unto all the inhabitants thereof." *

GROUP: Speak out, oh bell called Liberty,
           So we may understand
           The times you rang in freedom's name,
           Proclaimed it through the land.
           Speak out, oh bell of Liberty,
           So all of us may know
           The ways you spoke in freedom's name,
           Beginning long ago.

BOY: When I was young, I rang a lot!
           The times were tense and stirring,
           The thirteen colonies were roused
           By incidents occurring:
           I clanged alarms when England tried
           To force her taxes on us,
           I thundered when I saw the hand
           Of tyranny upon us!

GIRL: I whispered in a muffled voice,
           A voice of grief and mourning,

151

When Britain sent those hated Stamps
The colonists were scorning.

BOY: I roared with rage when Parliament
Forbade our people making
Iron and steel and woolen goods.
It seemed my lungs were breaking!

GIRL: I grieved for Boston when its port
Was closed to trade and shipping.
But though my muffled voice was sad,
My faith was far from slipping.

BOY: I called to citizens to come,
When Lexington was over,
And learn how farmers stood their ground
And Redcoats ran for cover.

BOY AND GIRL: With all my strength and all my heart
I called for folks' attendance
To hear the reading of the news
Declaring independence!

GIRL: And then I fell on silent days,
When I was put in hiding,
With Redcoats swarming in the streets
And British law presiding.

BOY: But I was back to shout about
Cornwallis's surrender.
I rang for freedom's victory,
I rang for freedom's splendor.

GIRL: For years I rang for this and that—
        A country in the making,
        The Constitution signed at last,
        And tasks for undertaking.
        And then I cracked . . .

GROUP: Your silent tongue
        Could never speak again,
        And yet your voice is loud and clear
        In all the minds of men!

        You stand upon your pedestal
        In Independence Hall,
        And all who come to visit you—
        The great, the old, the small—
        Receive a message from your heart
        Although your voice is still,
        For you proclaim our liberty,
        Oh bell . . . and always will.

ALL: "Proclaim liberty throughout all the land and
        unto all the inhabitants thereof." *

* These words are inscribed on the Liberty Bell.

Old Glory

It's more than stripes of red and white
And stars upon a field of blue—
The flag that waves so high and bright
Is dreams come true:
   Daring dreams of liberty,
   With minds and tongues and actions free.
It's more than color in the sun,
It's one for all and all for one!

It's more than red and white and blue,
A star to represent each state—
The flag that waves the day-hours through
Is faith grown great:
   Faith in basic rights of man
   On a democratic plan.
It's more than stripes that rise and fall,
It's all for one and one for all!

Thank You, America

(*This could be used as a choral reading with a different child for each section.*)

Thank you, America,
for our beautiful and spacious land,
our millions of acres of fields and wooded hills,
our forests and grasslands,
our mountains and treeless plains.
Thank you for our rivers and lakes,
and for the pattern of brooks flowing to the sea;
for two great oceans—on the east and west,
and two peaceful borders on the north and south.
Thank you, America, for all the beauty of this land.

And thank you, America, for abundance:
for the trees in our forests—hardwoods, softwoods,
that give us lumber for building houses and stores,
factories and furniture.
And thank you for the wild life in our forests,
and the fish in our streams;
and above all for the fertility of our soil
that enables us to produce so large a share
of the world's meat and cotton and corn and wheat.
And thank you for the riches under the earth—
silver and copper, gold and lead and zinc,
oil and coal, iron and uranium . . .

155

Thank you, America, for all this bounty we are blessed
with.

Thank you, America, for opportunity—
the open door, the rungs on the waiting ladder.
Thank you for the chance to live where we please,
to work where we want,
to own property, and manage our own affairs,
and to succeed or fail according to the way
we develop our abilities.

Thank you, America,
for our heritage of freedom and independence,
for ringing words that come out of the past
as strong as the day they were spoken:
"Give me liberty or give me death."
"Liberty and justice for all."
"Life, liberty, and the pursuit of happiness."
"From every mountain side let freedom ring."

Thank you, America, for the brave men
who signed the Declaration of Independence,
and for the far-sighted men
who framed the Constitution,
and for all the patriots—
known and unknown, young and old—
who worked to make our country strong
and its spirit invincible.

Thank you, America, for our Bill of Rights:
the right to freedom of speech and press,
and freedom to meet together as a group;
for the right to freedom of worship,

and security of person and property.
And thank you, not only for our rights,
but for the privilege of helping to pass them on intact
to those who follow us.

Thank you, America,
for your faith in us and in the future.
May we be given the foresight to care for the bounty
which you have entrusted to us
so that Americans who follow
will know the same plenty we are grateful for today.

Thank you, America,
for the past,
and the present,
and the future,
and help us to be worthy of our heritage.

Production Notes

A STAR FOR OLD GLORY

Characters: 3 male; 4 female.
Playing Time: 15 minutes.
Costumes: All characters wear costumes typical of the Revolutionary period.
Properties: Pattern of large, lopsided star; paper; scissors; one six-pointed star pattern made of two triangles; two five-pointed star patterns (the patterns may be pre-cut and then exhibited at the proper time); paper (flag resolution) and rough design of flag for Uncle George Ross.
Setting: The Ross upholstery shop. The room is furnished in the colonial manner. At one side are chairs and a sofa in the process of being repaired. A table and several chairs may also be in the room. Sewing equipment—needles, bolts of material, stuffing, twine, etc.—is placed around the room.
Lighting: No special effects.

SING, AMERICA, SING

Characters: 9 male; 3 female; any number of females for Girls Chorus, plus 3 or 4 to be cotton pickers; any number of males to take part in the various groups needed.
Playing Time: 30 minutes.
Costumes: The Narrator and the Stagehand wear everyday clothing. The Girls Chorus should be dressed in white blouses and dark skirts. Consult illustrated editions of song books and history books for other costumes.
Properties: Signs reading: New York, 1769; Chesapeake Bay, Sept., 1814; Boone's Farm, North Carolina, 1769; Any Town, U.S.A., Aug. 6, 1945. Coins; hats for the Sons of Liberty; pen and envelope for Francis Scott Key; sacks for Cotton Pickers; ropes for Cowboys; flags, horns, and possibly paper soldier caps and sunbonnets for the Chorus (as indicated in the text). Possible sound effects include train whistles, factory whistles, and a loudspeaker.
Setting: The stage may be bare or, if desired, there may be

chairs along the back of the stage for the Chorus.
Lighting: No special effects.

WASHINGTON MARCHES ON

Characters: 26 male; 7 female; male and female extras. (This is a maximum cast; many of the parts may be doubled up.)
Playing Time: 25 minutes.
Costumes: If costumes are used, all the characters should wear costumes appropriate for the time and place of their particular scenes.
Properties: Paper, ink, quill pen, packet of mail, map, magnifying glass, tripod, sewing, newspapers, knitting, letters, Bible, books, flags.
Setting: On stage are two chairs and a table holding paper, ink and quill pen. If a blackboard is used, it should be placed at a downstage corner of the stage.

WHEN FREEDOM WAS NEWS

Characters: 7 male; 3 female.
Playing Time: 25 minutes.
Costumes: The Newsstand Operator and Newsboy wear everyday, modern clothing. The Policeman wears a uniform and carries a stick. The boys and girls who are newspapers may wear everyday clothing; they also wear "sandwich boards" with the name of the paper and the date in large print, and the newspaper copy below.
Properties: Brick, coin container, newspapers, magazines, newspaper clippings.
Setting: The only necessary furnishing is a newsstand on one side of the stage. The stand is a typical sidewalk stand, with papers and magazines on display.
Lighting: If possible, a spot should play on the stand. The rest of the stage should be in semi-darkness to give a night atmosphere.

A DISH OF GREEN PEAS

Characters: 3 male; 2 female.
Playing Time: 25 minutes.
Costumes: The Orderly and Hickey wear uniforms. Van Starn wears farmer's clothing. Mattie and Miss Fraunces wear plain long-skirted dresses, aprons, and caps.
Properties: Scene 1: Various pieces of kitchen equipment, including bowls, spoons, etc.; basket of peas; bill. Scene 2: Pitcher; dish of peas; bottle of green liquid; glass; letter.
Setting: A colonial kitchen. The room is furnished with a table, chairs, cabinets and cooking equipment. At one side is a large fireplace. A kettle hangs in the fireplace. In Scene 2, the kettle holds

cooked peas.

Lighting: No special effects.

YANKEE DOODLE DANDY

Characters: 6 male; 2 female; male extras.

Playing Time: 10 minutes.

Costumes: The Tories are rather richly dressed in typical costumes of the period. The Recruits wear farm clothing and some may wear hats. 3rd Recruit has a big feather stuck in his hat.

Properties: None required.

Setting: No furnishings required. A backdrop of houses may be used.

Lighting: No special effects.

ASK MR. JEFFERSON

Characters: 3 male; 2 female.

Playing Time: 10 minutes.

Costumes: Modern, everyday dress for the students. Jefferson wears the typical dark suit and ruffled shirt of the period.

Properties: Notebooks, pencils for the students.

Setting: Scene 1 may be played before the curtain; no furnishings are necessary. Scene 2 is a library. There are several tables and chairs in the center of the room; bookcases filled with books line the walls. One table is covered with books, manuscripts and letters.

Lighting: No special effects.

"MOLLY PITCHER"

Characters: 3 male; 1 female; male extras.

Playing Time: 10 minutes.

Costumes: The Soldiers wear ragged uniforms and hats or worn work clothes. Molly wears a simple long-skirted dress.

Properties: Guns for the Soldiers; pitcher and cup for Molly.

Setting: Part of an orchard. A stone wall runs along part of the stage. Near the center is a fallen tree.